Accurate Business Forecasting

ACCURATE BUSINESS FORECASTING

A Harvard Business Review Paperback

ISBN 0-87584-291-7

The *Harvard Business Review* articles in this collection are available as individual reprints. Discounts apply to quantity purchases. For information and ordering contact Operations Department, Harvard Business School Publishing Division, Boston, MA 02163. Telephone: (617) 495-6192, 9 a.m. to 5 p.m. Eastern Time, Monday through Friday. Fax: (617) 495-6985, 24 hours a day.

Editor's Note: Some articles in this book may have been written before authors and editors began to take into consideration the role of women in management. We hope the archaic usage representing all managers as male does not detract from the usefulness of the collection.

Contents

*How to choose
the best technique –
or combination of
techniques –
to help solve your particular
forecasting dilemma*

Manager's guide to forecasting

*David M. Georgoff and
Robert G. Murdick*

One thing may be more certain for managers today than anything else: they have almost too much to think about and keep in mind in trying to assess problems realistically and solve them. Some respond by developing prejudices against any new idea because they don't have enough time to learn the new concepts properly. Others throw up their hands and admit they can't judge the idea with everything else they are handling.

Looking at forecasting at a time when they may need good forecasts more than ever, many managers are downplaying their importance. One reason may be that – like many other things – when forecasts are right, you don't hear about them. But when they're wrong....

In response to this problem, the authors have compiled a chart that profiles the 20 most common forecasting techniques and rates their attributes against 16 important evaluative dimensions. The result is a practical guide that will help executives sort out their priorities when choosing a technique and enable them to combine methods to achieve the best possible results.

Mr. Georgoff is professor of marketing at Florida Atlantic University and chairman of the Department of Management, Marketing, and International Business. He has published articles and worked as a consultant to large corporations in the areas of new product marketing, marketing planning, market research, and forecasting.

Mr. Murdick is professor of management at Florida Atlantic University. Previously he worked at the General Electric Company for 14 years. Well known in the field of management information systems, he is the author or coauthor of 18 books on management and marketing, the most recent of which is MIS: Concepts and Design *(Prentice-Hall, second edition, 1986).*

Early in 1984, the Houston-based COMPAQ Computer Corporation, manufacturer of IBM-compatible microcomputers, faced a decision that would profoundly affect its future. Recognizing that IBM would soon introduce its version of the portable computer and threaten COMPAQ's dominance in this profitable market, the company had two options. It could elect to specialize in this product line and continue to market its highly regarded portables aggressively, or it could expand market offerings to include desktop microcomputers. The latter move would force the year-old company to confront IBM on its home ground. Moreover, COMPAQ would have to make a substantial investment in product development and working capital and expand its organization and manufacturing capacity.

COMPAQ's management faced several important unknowns, including the potential market's size, structure, and competitive intensity. Management recognized that the company's vitality might seriously erode if it did not expand its product line. If the expansion were successful, COMPAQ might enjoy economies of scale that could help ensure its survival in a dynamic and very competitive industry. If COMPAQ's market assumptions were incorrect, however, its future might be bleak.

Many of today's managers face similar new market realities and uncertainties. Continually confronted with issues critical to their companies' competitive future, they must deal with novel and rapidly changing environments. In short, they must judge a broad range of dissimilar influences.

For more than a decade, new forecasting techniques have theoretically helped managers evaluate these varied factors. Much of the promise of

Authors' note: We thank Steven C. Wheelwright for his valuable assistance in the preparation of this article.

these techniques has been unrealized, however, even as a quickening succession of related advances have been overwhelming decision makers with new alternatives.

As the number of techniques proliferates, management also realizes that some of its crucial assumptions and projections about the economy have become quite tenuous. Equipped only with a little history, meager and questionable data, and frail and changing theoretical tools, the forecaster must nevertheless make critical decisions about altered futures.

As an example, COMPAQ Computer's quandary was further complicated because new technologies, competitors, and products were already transforming a market that had been only recently established. COMPAQ's forecast of the size, direction, and price trends of the 1984 microcomputer market was confounded by uncertainties about the market's response to several vital factors:

The entry of IBM's new portable computer.

IBM's 23% price cut in June 1984 and its potential erosion of margins.

The entry of lap portables introduced by Hewlett-Packard and Data General.

The launch of IBM's new PC AT, complicated by unexpected delivery delays and compatibility problems.

The introduction of desktop computers by Sperry, NCR, ITT, and AT&T.

Eventually, COMPAQ entered the desktop segment of the market, even though 1984 was unforgiving and rampageous. Several large competitors restricted their programs; many smaller companies went into—or to the edge of—receivership. Financially and competitively, COMPAQ succeeded. During 1984, sales rose from $111 million to $329 million and earnings increased from $4.7 million to $12.8 million.

The market's dynamics, however, make such results increasingly difficult to achieve; positive and negative events—both expected and unforeseen—have a decisive effect. Even when managers anticipate outcomes, grave uncertainties about timing, form, and impact persist.

Despite the difficulty, the vice president of marketing and the CEO—the two executives most directly involved with the decision—demonstrated what can be done. They used an extended series of consumer and dealer surveys coupled with periodic evaluations of the technology to assess the future market and to guide the development of products and programs

to accommodate the industry's fluid and rapidly evolving needs. Managers *can* use forecasting techniques to help them reach important decisions. A large and fast-growing body of research deals with the development, refinement, and evaluation of forecast techniques. Managers also have greater access to both internal and external data and can benefit from a multitude of computer software programs on the market, as well as easier access to computer capabilities for analyzing these data.

Forecaster's chart

While each technique has strengths and weaknesses, every forecasting situation is limited by constraints like time, funds, competencies, or data. Balancing the advantages and disadvantages of techniques with regard to a situation's limitations and requirements is a formidable but important management task.

We have developed a chart to help executives decide which technique will be appropriate to a particular situation; the chart groups and profiles a diverse list of 20 common forecasting approaches and arrays them against 16 important evaluative dimensions. We list techniques in columns and dimensions of evaluation in rows. Individual row-column intersections (cells) reflect our view of a technique's characteristics as they apply to each dimension. Brief descriptions of the forecasting methods are given on the chart.

We have used different colors to show which dimensions represent a strength for a particular technique and which represent its weaknesses. The strengths are highlighted in color; weaknesses are indicated by a gray cell. Naive extrapolation, for example, is strong in internal consistency in that it easily reflects changes in management decisions. It is weak, however, in forecast form. It is important to keep these distinctions in mind when you are using the chart.

The chart is useful in two ways. The first is in deciding which technique will suit your particular needs as a forecaster. The second is in deciding how to combine techniques to further improve the result. In this section, we discuss the simpler approach; we talk more about combining methods later.

To use the chart, look at the 16 questions listed in the first column after the dimensions. They are the most common questions a manager will ask when deciding to use a certain forecast. The first question sets out the various time spans a forecast would have to cover. Everyone who uses the chart will have to answer question 1. But each of the following questions can be answered with a yes or no. If you an-

Manager's guide to forecasting

Harvard Business Review
January–February 1986

swer no to a question, you don't have to look across that row.

In responding to question 1, make note of those techniques whose time span matches your needs. We have found it easiest for forecasters to write down the technique's column letter. The row number of each dimension and the column letter of each technique are written along the horizontal and vertical axes. With regard to question 1, for example, if your forecast horizon is short-term, you can write down the cell letters for naive extrapolation (A), sales-force composite (B), jury of executive opinion (C), and so forth. But you would ignore the letters for scenario methods (D), Delphi technique (E), historical analogy (F), and so on.

The columns you have now listed represent techniques that are qualified for further consideration. Next read down the column of each of these techniques and note any gray cells. If these gray cells are associated with questions to which you have answered yes, then the dimension either precludes use of the technique or the technique can be used but it has difficulty accommodating that dimension. Such precautions will help you determine whether you must—or wish to—eliminate certain techniques from further consideration. An arrow in a cell indicates that its evaluation is the same as the cell to its left.

After you have answered all the questions and have a list of surviving techniques, note the cells that are highlighted in color. Those cells represent specific strengths of a technique and can guide you in making a final selection.

In the course of the exercise, you may have eliminated a technique that you like, have heard about, or routinely use. You can go back to that one and compare its strengths and weaknesses with those of the methods that the chart has indicated would be best for you. You can then decide whether you would rather proceed with the technique that the chart indicates corresponds most closely to your specific requirements or whether you can accommodate the eliminating factors in order to use the technique that you initially favored.

Important considerations

When considering each question, you should remember some "tricks of the trade" concerning:

Time horizon. Most managers will want the forecast results to extend as far into the future as possible. Too long a period, however, may make the technique selection process even more confusing because of the varying abilities of the techniques to accommodate different time spans. In choosing an extended time horizon, the forecaster increases the complexity, cost, and time required to develop the final product.

You can break down the time needed to produce a forecast into development (Dev) and execution (Ex) time. Development time includes the gathering and entry of data, the modification of programs to the company's specific requirements, and the start-up of the system. Execution time is the time it takes to produce a forecast with a particular technique. Initially, of course, development time is a significant concern for the forecaster; once the forecast technique is firmly established, however, execution time is a more appropriate concern.

Technical sophistication. Experience shows that computer and mathematical sophistication is integral to many techniques. Although many executives have improved their skills in this area, not all have sharpened their quantitative skills enough to be comfortable with some of the forecast results a computer will spill out.

Cost. The cost of any technique is generally more important at the beginning when it is being developed and installed; after that, any technique's potential value to a decision maker usually exceeds the expense of generating an updated forecast.

Data availability. Before choosing a technique, the forecaster must consider the extensiveness, currency, accuracy, and representativeness of the available data. More data tend to improve accuracy, and detailed data are more valuable than those presented in the aggregate. Because a technique's ability to handle fluctuations is important to a forecast's success, the manager must match the sensitivity and stability of a technique to the random and systematic variability components of a data series.

Variability and consistency of data. Beyond changes that might occur in the company's structure or its environment, the manager must look at the kind of stable relationships assumed among a model's independent variables (represented by the "external stability" dimension). For example, while most historically oriented quantitative forecasts might use expected levels of automobile production as a basis for determining demand for steel, the forecast model may not reflect changes over time in the average amount of steel used in automobiles. These relationships sometimes do change, but any variation is usually so gradual that it will not affect a short-term forecast. When the forecasts are long-term, however, or when the company expects a substantial change in a vital relationship, the forecaster should either apply judgment in a quantitative technique or use a qualitative method.

Amount of detail necessary. While aggregate forecasts are easy to prepare, the manager will need specific information (including individual product classes, time periods, geographic areas, or product-market groupings, for example) to determine quotas or allocate resources. Since forecasts vary widely in their ability to handle such detail, the manager may want a technique that can accurately predict individual components and then combine the results into an overall picture. Otherwise, the forecaster can use one technique to provide an overall picture and then use past patterns or market factors to determine the component forecasts.[1]

Accuracy. While accuracy is a forecaster's holy grail, the maximum accuracy one can expect from a technique must fall within a range bounded by the average percentage error of the random component of a data series. Also, because of self-defeating and self-fulfilling prophecies, accuracy must be judged in light of the control the company has over the predicted outcome and within the time and resource constraints imposed on the forecaster.

Remember also that accuracy alone is not the most important criterion. The forecaster may wish to forgo some accuracy in favor of, for example, a technique that signals turning points or provides good supplemental information.

Turning points. Because turning points represent periods of exceptional opportunity or caution, the manager will want to analyze whether a technique anticipates fundamental shifts. Some techniques give false turn signals, so the forecaster must keep in mind not only a technique's ability to anticipate changes but also its propensity to give erroneous information.

Form. Final form varies greatly; it is always advisable to use a technique that provides some kind of mean or central value and a range of possible outcomes. If even remotely accurate, such information helps the manager determine more explicitly risk exposure, expected outcomes, and likelihood distributions.

Improving the forecast

Because no dramatic breakthroughs in technique development have occurred during the past several years, efforts to improve forecasts have shifted to searching for a better approach to technique selection. In part, these attempts have explored the strengths and performance characteristics of various techniques.[2] Our chart extends this approach by helping the forecaster match different techniques' strengths and characteristics to the needs and constraints of the required forecast.

Managers can improve their projection in the following ways:

Combining forecasts.

Simulating a range of input assumptions.

Selectively applying judgment.

Combining forecasts

The research on combining forecasts to achieve improvements (particularly in accuracy) is extensive, persuasive, and consistent.[3] The results of combined forecasts greatly surpass most individual projections, techniques, and analyses by experts. Because top-rated experts and the most popular techniques cannot consistently outperform an approach that combines results, and because the manager cannot predetermine which experts or techniques will be superior in any situation, combining forecasts—particularly with techniques that are dissimilar—offers the manager an assured way of improving quality.

The forecasting chart can help the manager select the best combination of techniques. As the chart shows, each method has strengths and weaknesses. By carefully matching two or more complementary techniques, the forecaster can offset any technique's limitations with the advantages of another, all the while retaining the strengths of the first. Simply compare an approach's highlighted cells against those of other qualified methods. Various techniques incorporate very different underlying notions. Not knowing which of these will ultimately prove to be most accurate in a particular economic environment, forecasters

1 For additional discussion, see G. David Hughes, "Sales Forecasting Requirements," in *The Handbook of Forecasting: A Manager's Guide*, ed. Spyros Makridakis and Steven C. Wheelwright (New York: John Wiley & Sons, 1982), p.13.

2 For a discussion of examples, see Spyros Makridakis et al., "The Accuracy of Extrapolation (Time Series) Methods," *Journal of Forecasting*, April-June 1982, p. 111; and Steven P. Schnaars, "Situational Factors Affecting Forecast Accuracy," *Journal of Marketing Research*, August 1984, p. 290.

3 See Essam Mahmoud, "Accuracy in Forecasting: A Survey," *Journal of Forecasting*, April-June 1984, p. 139; Spyros Makridakis and Robert L. Winkler, "Averages of Forecasts: Some Empirical Results," *Management Science*, September 1983, p. 987; and Victor Zarnowitz, "The Accuracy of Individual and Group Forecasts from Business Outlook Surveys," *Journal of Forecasting*, January-March 1984, p. 10.

can add to their awareness of possible outcomes by evaluating the range and the distribution of the projections produced by the various methods.[4]

part article on scenario forecasts by Pierre Wack in the September-October 1985 and November-December 1985 issues of HBR provides a good example of this. ⊟

Reprint 86104

Simulating various outcomes

The manager can also establish a range of probable outcomes by varying the combination and the levels of inputs of a particular technique. Such sensitivity analysis can underscore the most critical variables, the range and distribution of expected outcomes, and the probable outcomes from different assumptions.

Using judgment

While many quantitative forecasts incorporate some subjectivity, forecasters should rely more heavily on the output of a quantitative forecast than on their own judgment. Forecasting research has concluded that even simple quantitative techniques outperform the unstructured intuitive assessments of experts and that using judgment to adjust the values of a quantitatively derived forecast will reduce its accuracy.[5] This is so because intuitive predictions are susceptible to bias and managers are limited in their ability to process information and maintain consistent relationships among variables.[6]

The forecaster should incorporate subjective judgments in dynamic situations when the quantitative models do not reflect significant internal and external changes. Even in these cases, the forecaster should incorporate the subjective adjustments as inputs in the model rather than adjusting the model's final outcome.

When confronted with extended horizons or with novel situations that have limited data and no historical precedent, judgment or counting methods should be used. Applying judgment in such situations, however, should be done on a structured basis. The forecaster should also employ judgment to stimulate thought and explore new relationships but, where possible, quantitative techniques should be incorporated to test and support assumptions. The two-

4 See Hillel J. Einhorn and Robin M. Hogarth, "Prediction, Diagnosis, and Causal Thinking," *Journal of Forecasting*, January-March 1982, p. 23.

5 For survey articles that address this issue, see Mahmoud, p. 139; and Robin M. Hogarth and

Spyros Makridakis, "Forecasting and Planning: An Evaluation," *Management Science*, February 1981, p. 115.

6 Lennart Sjoberg, "Aided and Unaided Decision Making: Improved Intuitive Judgment," *Journal of Forecasting*, October-December 1982, p. 349.

Decision analysis comes of age

No longer the exclusive toy of management scientists, decision analysis is becoming an accepted managerial tool for solving everyday business problems

Jacob W. Ulvila and Rex V. Brown

Ten years ago, decision analysis was still an experimental management technique. But even then supporters claimed that eventually it would become for the manager what calculus is to the engineer. According to the authors of this article, decision analysis that incorporates personal judgment has not yet become what some expected, but it has, nonetheless, gained acceptance in many large corporations and government departments. One of the reasons for this acceptance is the greater flexibility and sensitivity of decision analysis to managers' needs than earlier forms had. In other words, today's decision analysis techniques can better take into account the people, the politics, the time pressures, and all the messy but critical factors that managers have to contend with. In this article, the authors describe three major forms of decision analysis and show how real managers have used decision tree analysis, probabilistic forecasting, and multiattribute analysis to solve real business problems.

Mr. Ulvila is vice president of Decision Science Consortium, Inc., a management consulting firm based in Falls Church, Virginia. He specializes in the application of decision analysis and other quantitative methods to a variety of problem areas, especially business planning. Mr. Brown is chairman of the board of Decision Science Consortium, Inc. Formerly on the faculty of Harvard Business School, he is author or coauthor of four books on decision analysis and marketing, including Decision Analysis for the Manager *(New York: Holt, Rinehart & Winston, 1974). This is his second article in HBR.*

In the early 1970s, C. Jackson Grayson, onetime head of the Wage and Price Commission and also author of one of the first books on applied decision analysis, urged analysts to "put people, time, power, data accessibility, and response time into models and create crude, workable solutions" if they wanted busy people like himself to use them.[1]

At the time, decision analysis was still an experimental management technique, a fairly straightforward application of statistical decision theory.[2] The choice facing a decision maker was expressed as a mathematical function of probability and utility numbers, which measured the person's uncertainties and value judgments. (The best option was the one with the highest expected utility.) Although decision analysis was well established as a way to quantify logically the considerations that go into any choice among options, it had just begun to move out of the business schools and into practical application in the business world. Only a handful of corporations provided in-house expertise, and consultants specializing in decision analysis were rarely called on.

Now, after ten years of sometimes humbling feedback from the real world, analysts have learned to be more flexible and modest in how to make the basic decision theory formulation useful to managers. The technology has been enhanced to capture more considerations relevant to sound decision making, notably through multiattribute utility analysis and improved interaction with the user. Decision analysis has emerged as a complement to older decision-making techniques such as systems modeling and operations research. In addition to statistical decision theory, the new technology draws on psychology, economics, and social science.

Editor's note: All references are listed at the end of the article on page 141.

What is retained and is distinctive about the approach is that the quantitative models incorporate personal judgments. To distinguish this approach from other ways of analyzing decisions in widespread use (such as those that depend only on "objective" inputs), we call it personalized decision analysis.

Analysts have learned to use the data and expertise that are immediately available to the decision maker and to play back conclusions to the manager in close to real time. In 1970, an analysis was rarely completed within three months. Now, meaningful analysis of a problem can be generated in an afternoon, and a succession of analyses can be presented in intervals of one or two days. Without greatly disturbing their schedule of meetings or reflective process, managers can now respond to these analyses and provide input for other rounds.

Although such decision analysis has not become the dominant analytic discipline that some people expected, its use has grown dramatically since 1970. Personalized decision analysis has become an accepted part of the staff services that major corporations draw on routinely, much as they do industrial psychology, cost analysis, marketing research, and economic analysis. And virtually all the major areas of government have adopted decision analysis in one form or another.

The case studies that we present in this article illustrate how managers use the three major variants of decision analysis currently in use—decision tree analysis, probabilistic forecasting, and multiattribute utility analysis.

Decision tree analysis

Decision tree analysis is the oldest and most widely used form of decision analysis. Managers have used it in making business decisions in uncertain conditions since the late 1950s, and its techniques are familiar.[3] Over the past several years, however, the manner in which people conduct decision tree analysis has expanded. Today's analyst has at his or her disposal not only an array of computer supports that make quick turnaround possible but also the accumulated wisdom of analysts over the last 20 years. The following case illustrates some of the components of a successful decision tree analysis. They include the use of simple displays, sensitivity analysis to guide refinements, and subsidiary models to ensure completeness. Also important are the direction and integration the analysis gives to the contributions of experts as well as the involvement of top managers.

Should AIL purchase rights to a new patent?

Late in 1974, the AIL Division of Cutler-Hammer, Inc. (now a division of Eaton Corporation) was offered the opportunity to acquire the defense market rights to a new flight-safety system patent. The inventor claimed he had a strong patent position as well as technical superiority, but the market for the product was very uncertain, mostly because of pending legislative action. Because the inventor wished to make an offer to other companies if AIL was not interested, he asked AIL to make the decision in a few weeks, a period of time clearly inadequate to resolve any uncertainties it was aware of.

AIL had not used formal decision analysis before. Top managers were, however, familiar with the theory and its typical applications through the literature and interested in trying these techniques on an actual decision to evaluate their worth. The patent decision appeared to be a good candidate for such a trial.

A team of AIL personnel and outside analysts spent two weeks developing an analysis of the patent idea. All the while, the team stayed in continual contact with top management.

AIL's analysis

The analysts used standard decision tree techniques. *Exhibit I* shows the immediate choice, to purchase a six-month option on the patent rights or not, and the main uncertainties that affected the decision. The attractiveness of each outcome, or path through the tree, is represented by its present-value earnings. These range from a loss of $700,000 to a gain of $10.5 million. The expected value at each node in the tree is calculated by taking a probability-weighted average of its branches. Working these values gives an expected value of $100,425. That is, AIL could expect to be better off by $100,425 if it purchased the six-month option.

The mechanics of the analysis—specifying the tree, assigning values, and calculating results—are straightforward. The usefulness of the analysis, however, depends more on how the analysis process is managed than on the mechanics. Five features that are often absent in unsuccessful attempts to apply decision analysis marked this implementation as a success.

A simple display. The focus of the analysis was the simple tree shown in *Exhibit I*. The most common mistake that a beginner at decision analysis makes is to include everything the choice involves in the tree. This is a sure way to end up with a mess, which only the analyst, if anyone, can under-

Exhibit I   **AIL's decision tree**

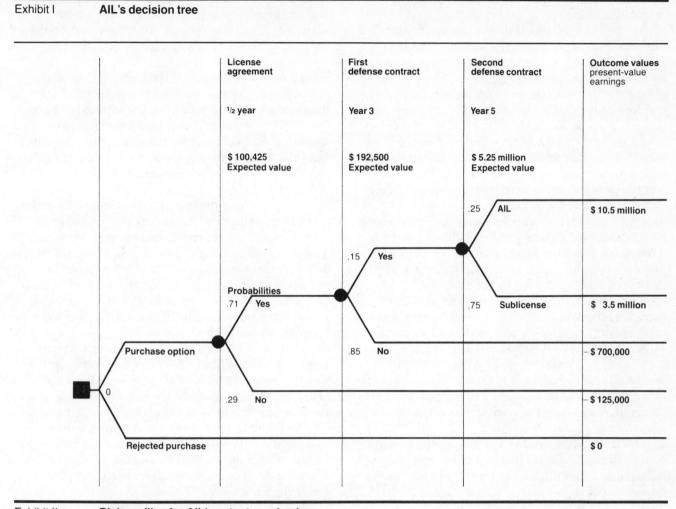

| | License agreement | First defense contract | Second defense contract | Outcome values present-value earnings |

License agreement — ½ year — $100,425 Expected value

First defense contract — Year 3 — $192,500 Expected value

Second defense contract — Year 5 — $5.25 million Expected value

.25 AIL → $10.5 million

.15 Yes

.75 Sublicense → $3.5 million

Probabilities
.71 Yes

.85 No → –$700,000

Purchase option

.29 No → –$125,000

0

Rejected purchase → $0

Exhibit II   **Risk profiles for AIL's patent purchasing decision**
distribution of incremental discounted earnings in millions of dollars

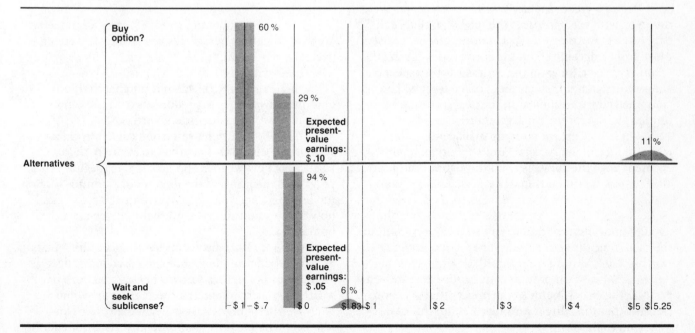

Alternatives

Buy option?
60 %
29 %
Expected present-value earnings: $.10
11 %

Wait and seek sublicense?
94 %
Expected present-value earnings: $.05
6 %

–$1 –$.7 $0 $.83 $1 $2 $3 $4 $5 $5.25

stand. Such a tree is unlikely to influence any manager's decision.

The trick is to design a simple tree that captures the essence of the problem by including its most important elements. In this case, the most important elements affecting earnings were the probabilities of exercising the option, receiving an initial contract, and continuing on a second contract.

Refining the elements. By means of an interactive computer program, the analysts determined how sensitive the results were to changes in the inputs to the tree. The analysis was then expanded in a way that would be most responsive to what the decision maker needed to know.

Use of subsidiary models. The analysts at AIL developed models to refine estimates of the most sensitive inputs. Using a simple tree does not make the analysis coarse or incomplete; subsidiary models can ensure any desired level of detail and sophistication. In this case, the analysts used three subsidiary models. They used one to determine yearly earnings and calculate present values and another to assess the probability of receiving a contract.

The latter model reflected important factors such as the timing and terms of a possible legislative mandate for the system, the strength of possible competitive systems, and the likelihood of a crash or near crash of a plane within the next several months. The analysts used a third model to assess probability distributions of earnings from the contracts that reflected uncertainties in the number of units, the price per unit, and the profit margin. Each subsidiary model was compact and could be displayed on a single chart, which the analysts used to answer top managers' questions about how the figures in the main model had been determined.

Team input. At AIL various people were involved with each aspect of the model, so that each expert could focus on the area of his expertise. Those most knowledgeable about the chances of winning the second contract, for example, addressed this aspect of the problem but did not consider other aspects. The combined contributions of all the experts formed a unified picture for top management.

Contact with top management. The most important factor was the close work of top management with the analysis team throughout the analysis. This interaction ensured that:

1   The choices modeled were in fact the choices under consideration. (In this case, as a result of the modeling, the analysts identified a new choice – waiting and seeking a sublicense.)

2   All important concerns were addressed. For AIL, the issues included the impact that decision factors other than direct earnings have (in this case, return on capital).

3   The level of modeling was right. That is, some aspects were modeled formally, but others were left to informal consideration. For example, the analysts explored AIL's attitude toward risk taking by displaying risk profiles of the choices rather than by assessing and using a utility function.[4] (Because answering the hypothetical questions about preferences for uncertain returns that are required to establish a utility function strikes many managers as gambling, many of them are reluctant to do it. In this case, the uncertainties of the decision could be sufficiently characterized in simple risk profiles.)

Exhibit II shows the risk profiles of the alternatives AIL faced. Purchasing the option would give an expected net present value of earnings of about $100,000, a 60% chance of losing about $700,000, a 29% chance of losing about $125,000, and an 11% chance of having a positive return from a distribution with an expectation of about $5.25 million. (This picture corresponds to a more detailed analysis of the earnings from a defense contract.)

The alternative, waiting and seeking a sublicense, would have a 94% chance of producing no gain (or loss) and a 6% chance of producing a distribution with an expectation of about $830,000 and would result in an expected value of about $50,000. This display facilitated a unanimous decision by the decision-making group (the president and his vice presidents for business development and operations) to go with the less risky strategy even though it offered a slightly lower expected value.

Other companies' experiences

Companies in a wide range of industries are using decision tree analysis to make a variety of decisions. For example:

☐   Through this kind of analysis, Ford has determined whether to produce its own tires and whether to stop producing convertibles.

☐   The defense systems division of Honeywell uses decision tree analysis to evaluate the attractiveness of new weapons programs. On a regular basis, program managers and the director of planning develop models to help decide which programs to pursue and how they should allocate internal research and development funds.

☐   With decision tree analysis, Pillsbury's grocery products division has evaluated major decisions, such as whether to switch from a box to a bag for a certain grocery product. In this case, even when analysts used pessimistic assessments expressed by a manager who initially recommended remaining with the box, the analysis showed that the profitability would be greater with the bag. The analysis also showed that the value of making a market test, as urged by some executives, could not remotely approach its cost. The bag was introduced, and the profits on the product climbed.

☐   Faced with a decision to electrify part of its system, which would involve capital expenditures of several hundred million dollars, Southern Railway carried out an analysis that gave managers a better understanding of the interactions of variables influencing the decision.

☐   Many major oil and gas companies, such as Union Texas Petroleum, the Champlin oil and gas subsidiary of Union Pacific, and Gulf Oil, apply decision analysis regularly to choose appropriate sites for exploration and evaluate the economics of field development.

☐   ITT uses decision analysis at many levels of the company, especially for capital investment decisions.

Probabilistic forecasting

The previous section illustrates how personalized decision analysis can capture all the thinking that goes into a particular decision. The technique has other uses as well. Analysts can develop certain aspects of decision analysis into analytic tools that can be used in a variety of contexts. Analysts can use the probabilistic modeling aspects of decision analysis to develop forecasts of, for instance, future sales and profits, which in turn can be used to support decisions about planning, investment, and marketing. Developing a single aspect of personalized decision analysis to support decisions in a variety of contexts is likely to become very popular. Because its cost can be spread over many uses, a company can afford to use enough computerization and staff time to do this type of analysis properly.

The following example illustrates how personalized decision analysis can be used for forecasting. Of course, this kind of analysis is not the only way to carry out quantitative forecasting. What is distinctive about this approach's contribution to the problem is that, rather than limit a forecast to statistical extrapolation from the past, it can combine assessments of judgment with data. In cases where little or no relevant history is available on which to base a forecast and where each product's success depends on a combination of events about which personal judgment is virtually the only source of information, this form of analysis is particularly helpful.

How will Honeywell's defense division grow?

In late 1979, the manager of planning for the defense systems division of Honeywell, Inc. faced the task of planning the division's growth over the next ten years. A major part of the work involved finding how to stay within the R&D budget and yet pursue new product opportunities to increase the division's sales and profits.

After he screened the new product opportunities according to their fit with the rest of the division, the manager needed forecasts of the products' sales, profits, and investment requirements. The products' successful development, the strength of competition, and their eventual market success were all uncertain. In addition, the chances for success of some of the products were interrelated, and several products offered the chance of significant collateral business.

The approach the analysts took was to build a composite forecast for the division by combining decision tree analyses of individual products. During the project, Honeywell's planners worked closely with decision analysis consultants and, by the time they had finished, had acquired the skills needed to carry out the analyses in-house. This type of analysis is now a regular part of Honeywell's project evaluation, planning, and forecasting activity.

The analysts developed a model for each product along lines similar to AIL's. The analysis team worked closely with each project manager and his staff to build the decision tree, assess probabilities and values, and discuss results and sensitivities.

The two analyses differed significantly, however, in a number of ways. First, the results of Honeywell's analysis were to be used for forecasting as well as for decision making. This use meant that the analysts would need to model additional factors and would have to make the form the outputs took suitable for forecasting.

Second, because the success of some products was related to the the success of others, the analysts had to include in the analysis such factors as common investments, collateral business opportunities, and marketing interactions.

Third, Honeywell's problem presented no clear single criterion according to which management could make a decision. Honeywell considered several financial criteria such as internal rate of return, net present value, and yearly streams of profits, investments, and return on investment.

Honeywell's forecasts
Exhibit III shows the probabilistic sales forecast for one group of interrelated products. This

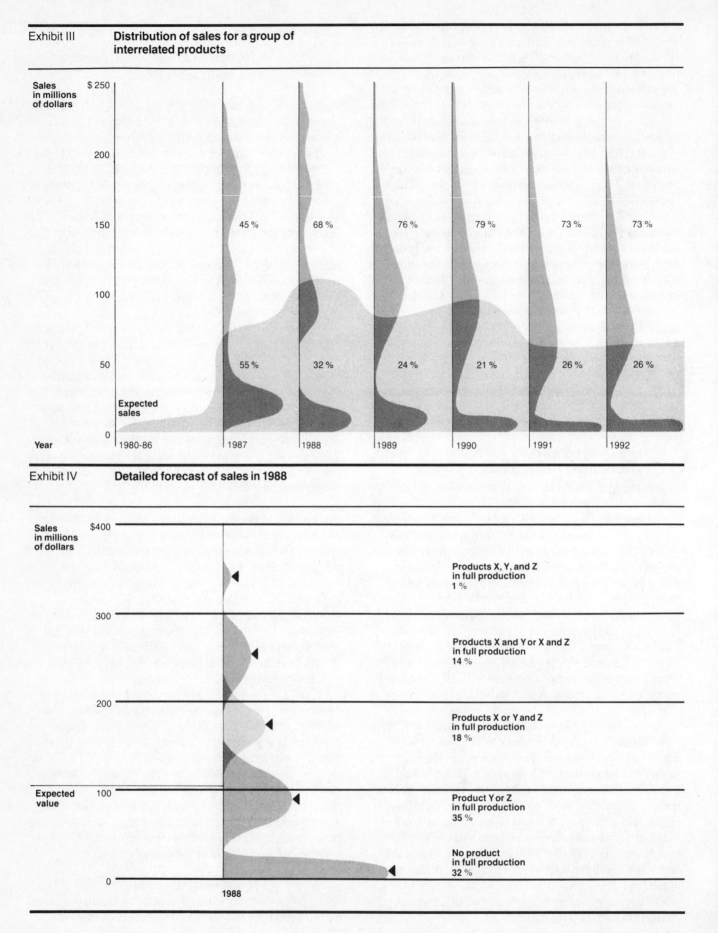

Exhibit III   **Distribution of sales for a group of
interrelated products**

Sales in millions of dollars

$ 250

200

150

45 %   68 %   76 %   79 %   73 %   73 %

100

50

55 %   32 %   24 %   21 %   26 %   26 %

Expected sales

0

Year   1980-86   1987   1988   1989   1990   1991   1992

Exhibit IV   **Detailed forecast of sales in 1988**

Sales in millions of dollars

$400

Products X, Y, and Z
in full production
1 %

300

Products X and Y or X and Z
in full production
14 %

200

Products X or Y and Z
in full production
18 %

Expected value   100

Product Y or Z
in full production
35 %

No product
in full production
32 %

0

1988

forecast is based on decision tree analyses of three main products and two collateral business opportunities. The analysts first developed decision trees for each product to determine the distributions of sales in the event that a market sufficient to support full production both did and did not emerge. Then they developed a second level of analysis to model the key interdependencies among the products; specifically, the probability of any particular product being in full production depended on which other products were also in full production.

The forecast shows that low sales are expected from the products for the first seven years. After that, sales for the next six years are expected to be about $75 million per year. This amount is not certain, however. The forecast, for instance, shows a 24% chance of sales being below $25 million in 1989.

The supporting decision tree analyses were useful for explaining the shape of each year's forecast. *Exhibit IV* shows that because of uncertainty about which products would have sufficient markets to support full production by 1988, the forecast for sales is "lumpy." The reasons for these uncertainties are detailed in the decision tree analyses.

This analysis helped Honeywell to assess the chances that these products would meet sales goals, the uncertainties in the assessment, and the reasons for the uncertainties. By detailing the chain of events that would produce different levels of sales, it also identified points of leverage—places where Honeywell could take action to change probabilities and improve sales.

The analysts also used the decision trees to forecast yearly profits, fund flows, assets, research and development investments, and the related financial quantities of net present value, internal rate of return, and annual return on investment. Their forecasts indicated that these products could be expected to exceed requirements on all factors and that, unless Honeywell was very risk averse, they were attractive.

Honeywell's managers compared forecasts to decide which product opportunities to pursue. These comparisons provided an additional screen since some products were clearly worse than others on *all* factors. But because the analysis didn't show the relative importance of each factor—some products were projected to perform better on certain factors (for example, internal rate of return and net present value) and other products were projected to perform better on other factors (for example, return on investment)—an unambiguous ordering of the products was impossible. Honeywell's managers might have had such an ordering if their analysts had used some of the newer techniques of multiattribute utility.

Multiattribute utility analysis

In trying to determine where to place its European subsidiary, the top management of one company completely ignored a decision tree analysis that showed careful consideration of the financial implications of possible locations. When pressed for an explanation, top management confided that the choice was dominated by the fact that key personnel wanted to be near the International School in Geneva. Somehow, that consideration seemed too noneconomical and nonrational to be included in the analysis—yet it did dominate the decision. At the time the decision was made, the technology of decision analysis was ill equipped to handle the trade-offs between financial effects and intangibles. A new technique, multiattribute utility analysis, makes such modeling possible by precisely specifying the factors that affect the choice, making trade-offs among the factors, and choosing the alternative that offers the best balance.

Multiattribute utility analysis evolved out of decision analysis that supported government decisions, in which the need to balance multiple objectives is most obvious. As the case of the company deciding where to put its plant shows, however, its usefulness for business decision making is evident. For example, plant sites usually differ in such intangibles as the skill of the local work force, the ability of local management, and the management problems of operating plants in the locations under consideration. These are important factors to consider in the decision of where to locate the plant, yet it is virtually impossible to specify their impact on profit with any precision.

Many factors also arise in strategic decisions. For example, Michael E. Porter has argued that, when considering the strategic decisions of vertical integration, major capacity expansion, and entry into new businesses, managers should go beyond cost and investment analyses to consider broad strategic issues and perplexing administrative problems and that these are very hard to quantify.[5] Multiattribute utility analysis, which is illustrated in the following case, provides a way to quantify and trade off such factors.

Which bomb detection system should the FAA choose?

Over the past few years, the Federal Aviation Administration has been supporting research and development on a system to detect bombs in airplane

Exhibit V   **Hierarchy of attributes in the FAA's analysis**
in preference weights

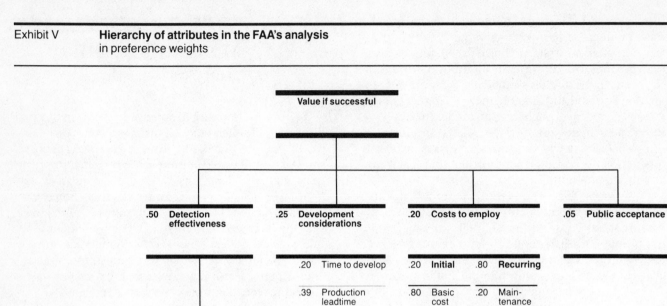

	Value if successful				
.50	Detection effectiveness	.25 Development considerations	.20 Costs to employ	.05 Public acceptance	

	Development considerations		Costs to employ		
.20	Time to develop	.20	Initial	.80	Recurring
.39	Production leadtime	.80	Basic cost	.20	Maintenance
.39	Operating size	.20	Competition	.65	Operating personnel
.02	Transportability			.15	Consumables

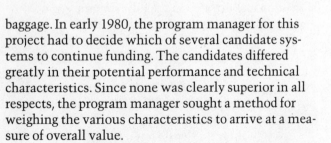

	Explosive A		Explosive B		Explosive C		Other explosives
.40		.40		.18		.02	
.75	Standard bomb	.75	Standard bomb	.75	Standard bomb		
.80	5% chance of false alarm	.81	5% chance of false alarm	.80	5% chance of false alarm		
.20	1% chance of false alarm	.20	1% chance of false alarm	.20	1% chance of false alarm		
.25	Smaller	.25	Smaller	.25	Smaller		

baggage. In early 1980, the program manager for this project had to decide which of several candidate systems to continue funding. The candidates differed greatly in their potential performance and technical characteristics. Since none was clearly superior in all respects, the program manager sought a method for weighing the various characteristics to arrive at a measure of overall value.

A team of outside analysts worked closely with the program manager and other FAA personnel to develop a comprehensive model of the value of each system. To determine an efficient allocation of budgeted funds, they combined these values with assessments of the probabilities of success and development costs.

The FAA's analysis

The analysts' primary goal was to develop a comprehensive model for evaluating and comparing candidates. This development involved four activities—defining attributes of value, assessing performance of the candidates on each attribute, determining trade-offs across attributes, and calculating overall values.[6]

Defining preference attributes. The analysts sought to define attributes with four characteristics. The attributes were to be comprehensive enough to account for most of what is important in evaluating the candidates, to highlight the differences among the candidates, to reflect separate, nonoverlapping values to avoid double counting, and to be independent of each other.

When the analysts had identified attributes that satisfied these four requirements, they then arranged the attributes in a hierarchy showing the logical relationships among attributes. This is shown in *Exhibit V.*

The first main attribute is the effectiveness of the device at detecting bombs. This is subdivided into the type of explosive, the size of the bomb, and the detection-false alarm ratio.

The second main attribute, development considerations, is divided into four subcategories—time to develop a prototype, production lead time, operating size (which would determine a system's location in an airport), and transportability.

Cost to employ the system in an airport, the third main attribute, is divided into initial costs and recurring costs. Initial costs reflect a basic cost estimate based on technical considerations and an estimate of the effects of competition. Recurring costs include maintenance, operating personnel, and material consumed during operation.

The fourth main attribute is the system's acceptability to passengers.

Assessing performance of candidates on each attribute. To assess preference, the analysts required scales for all attributes. They used two types of measure—scales with natural standard units (including dollars for costs, months or hours for time, and percentages for detection rates) and relative scales. Wherever possible, the performance of a candidate was first assessed in natural units. These assessments were then transformed into 0-to-100-point scales for standardization. The candidate with the best performance (the lowest cost, for example) received a score of 100; the one with the worst performance (the highest cost, for instance) received a score of 0; and the others received intermediate scores.

Where no natural measure existed (for example, for "public acceptance"), performance was assessed directly on a 0-to-100-point scale. Again, a score of 100 was assigned to the candidate with the best performance, 0 to the worst performance, and so forth.

Exhibit VI	**Performance of the FAA's bomb detection candidates on development considerations** on a scale of 0 to 100					
				Candidates		
Development considerations	A	B	C	D	E	F
Time to develop	100	50	0	62	50	25
Production leadtime	50	100	75	50	0	50
Operating size	100	100	50	100	0	100
Transportability	100	100	100	100	0	60

Exhibit VI shows, for instance, the scores for the six candidates on each development consideration. Candidate A was assessed to have the best "time to develop" since it was fully developed at the time of the analysis. It was assigned a value of 100. Candidate C would take the longest time to develop—four years. It received a value of 0. Other candidates would take intermediate amounts of time to develop and thus received intermediate scores.

Determining trade-offs across attributes. By assessing a set of weights to represent the decision maker's judgment about the relative importance of improving performance from the worst to the best level for each attribute, analysts could determine trade-offs across attributes. The analysts assessed the weights by referring to the range of performance the scales reflected instead of to abstract notions of importance.

Consider, for example, the weights of the development considerations shown in *Exhibit V.* For these attributes, the ranges of possible variation in "production lead time" (18 months) and in "operating size" were considered most important. The variation of "time to develop" (4 years) was assessed to be half as important (as important as a variation of 9 months on "production lead time"). Finally, the variation of "transportability" (32 hours) was assessed to be one-tenth as important as "time to develop" (or about as important as 5 months of development time). These assessments are represented by weights that are in the ratios of .5:1:1:.05 for time to develop, production lead time, operating size, and transportability. Normalized weights of .20:.39:.39:.02 (which retain these ratios) were used for standardization.

The analysts assessed weights both directly, as we explained earlier, and indirectly. They used an indirect method to assess the weight between initial and recurring costs. This method determined weights that were consistent with a 10% discount rate and a ten-year operating horizon.

Calculating overall values. The fourth modeling activity was to calculate a weighted-average score for each candidate by working up through the hierarchy. Thus, using the values in *Exhibit VI* and the weights in *Exhibit V*, analysts calculated the value of candidate A on "development considerations" as:

$$(100)(.20) + (50)(.39) + (100)(.39) + (100)(.02) \simeq 80.$$

Similar calculations produced the values for the candidates on each main attribute that are shown in *Exhibit VII*. The analysts next calculated the overall value of each candidate by taking a weighted average of these scores. For example, the overall value of candidate A is:

$$(57)(.50) + (80)(.25) + (82)(.20) + (70)(.05) \simeq 68.$$

Overall value is a measure of the attractiveness of each candidate that can be compared with measures for other candidates. The result of the analysis shows that candidate B offers the best balance of characteristics, that candidates C and D are almost as attractive, and that candidates E and F offer the worst balances.

The value of the analysis

The FAA's primary use of the analysis was to quantify each candidate's value in a way that permitted comparison. To determine an efficient allocation of R&D funds, the analysts combined these evaluations with estimates of each candidate's probability of success and cost of development.

The FAA's analysis also facilitated several aspects of the decision-making process. First, it helped resolve disagreements. The disaggregation of the elements of the decision clarified the source of a disagreement—was it about facts (for example, the cost of a system) or a difference in judgment (for instance, the relative importance of cost in comparison with detection performance)? Once the disagreements were clear, managers could deal with them by, for example, gathering additional supporting information. If the disagreement persisted, the model could determine its importance. For each input, the model could show whether the disagreement significantly affected the overall evaluation. Even if a disagreement was significant, the model at least isolated its cause. This clarification enabled the ultimate decision maker to make a better judgment.

The disaggregation also allowed the analyst to make a comprehensive analysis of the candidates. The team could investigate each attribute thoroughly yet keep its contribution to the overall evaluation in perspective. This arrangement prevented the analysts from wasting attention on unimportant issues.

To give a balanced picture of the whole, the multiattribute analysis synthesized the various pieces of the assessment. The analysts considered the impact of all important factors before they came up with a recommendation.

Business use of multiattribute utility analysis

Multiattribute utility analysis has been used widely to aid government decision makers. For instance, it has been used to select military systems, set water-supply policy, site nuclear facilities, allocate nuclear inspection resources, determine fire department operations, evaluate crime-prevention programs, and prepare international negotiators.

Its use as an aid in making business decisions has not been as widespread, but the next few years should see a dramatic increase. Multiattribute analysis is useful for any decision in which multiple factors are important, no alternative is clearly best on all factors, and some factors are difficult to quantify. Several business decisions have these characteristics:

Where to put a plant. Sites often differ in many important aspects. Some factors, such as differences in capital costs (land, plant, and equipment) and in operating revenue and expenses (access to markets, labor rates, tax benefits, shipping costs), are easily reduced to financial terms. Other factors that may be crucial to the decision are more difficult to reduce to dollars. These include the availability and skill of local labor, the degree of unionization, the difficulty of managing geographically dispersed units, and legal restrictions on operations. Multiattribute analysis can highlight the sources of differences and enable managers to make quantitative trade-offs between financial factors and "intangibles."

Whether to integrate vertically. A decision to integrate an operation or not requires that management consider a multitude of factors, many of which are difficult to quantify with standard financial techniques: access to new information, access to new technologies, ability to control specifications of products or raw materials, economies of combined operations, difficulty in balancing "upstream" and "downstream" units, and increased fixed costs of doing business.

Whether and how to enter a new business. This decision can involve considerations that are often ignored in capital budgeting:

The production or marketing "fit" between new and existing businesses or technologies.

Exhibit VII	**Overall value of candidates** on a scale of 0 to 100							
		Candidates					
Attribute category	Preference weight	A	B	C	D	E	F
Detection effectiveness	.50	57	72	88	62	39	0
Other development considerations	.25	80	90	51	73	10	65
Costs to employ	.20	82	91	88	87	39	70
Public acceptance	.05	70	90	90	85	0	100
	Overall value	68	81	79	71	30	35

Special skills or technologies required to operate the new business.

"Cultural fit" between new and old businesses (especially important if entry is by acquisition).

Relative strengths of competitors in the new business.

By using multiattribute utility analysis, managers can balance these factors against financial considerations to derive a comprehensive evaluation of alternatives.

What and whether to negotiate. Many negotiations—labor, real estate, and sales, for example—may involve several issues. A labor negotiation could include issues of wage rates, length of agreement, grievance procedures, work rules, seniority, job security, union security, vacations, fringe benefits, and pension fund contributions. Both sides' opening positions on the issues are often clear, but how they view the trade-offs across issues is not. Using multiattribute analyses of their own preferences and trade-offs and those of the other side, negotiators can uncover opportunities to give a small concession in return for a large benefit.[7]

How to allocate research and development budgets. Research and development projects often exhibit a variety of performance characteristics that managers may need to balance to determine the best project. Multiattribute utility analysis can help them do this. They can also combine such an analysis with a decision tree analysis to address uncertainties and risks.

The forecast for decision analysis

If the trends of the past decade continue at their present rate, then over the next decade we can certainly expect to see personalized decision analysis spread and become firmly established as a staff function throughout industry. Virtually all corporations of any substance will have in-house staffs or outside consultants to analyze decisions and report findings to top management.

The big question is, however, whether decision analysis will become an integrated part of management's decision making. As C. Jackson Grayson has persuasively argued, the integration requires that the cultural gap between management scientists and managers be bridged. Without the bridge, personalized decision analysis, like operations research and other analytic techniques, may never be more than an optional aid, albeit interesting.

For the integration to take place, managers will have to become more skilled at using decision analysis and its practitioners more effective than they are now. In other words, analysts and managers-to-be need to undergo extensive training in the integration of decision analysis with existing organizational and personal decision processes. (This training would go far beyond the teaching of particular techniques, which is as far as most business schools go now.) The integration may also require organizational changes in control and reward structures in business.

At present, appropriate professional training is not readily available to either the manager or the specialized decision analyst. What is needed is a course of study (and supporting research) that integrates the logical, the psychological, and the organizational aspects of applied subjective decision analysis. This will probably not become available until there is at least one institute of research and teaching devoted to all aspects of decision-aiding technology (including personalized analysis) and to their integration.

This training would require overcoming the institutional rigidities associated with partitioning universities along such traditional departmental lines as engineering, psychology, business, and statistics. Even within single departments such as business, the feeder disciplines—organizational behavior, applied mathematics, finance, business policy, and marketing—are usually kept jealously apart. If these can be adequately synthesized, management science in general, and personalized decision analysis in particular, can at last achieve full-fledged assimilation into the day-to-day business of management. ▽

Reprint 82511

References

1 See C. Jackson Grayson,
Decisions Under Uncertainty
(Boston: Division of Research,
Harvard University Graduate School of
Business Administration, 1960)
and "Management Science and
Business Practice,"
HBR July-August 1973, p. 41.

2 See Rex V. Brown,
"Do Managers Find Decision Theory Useful?"
HBR May-June 1970, p.78,
and Howard Raiffa and Robert O. Schlaifer,
Applied Statistical Decision Theory
(Boston: Division of Research,
Harvard University Graduate School of
Business Administration, 1962).

3 See, for example, John F. Magee,
"Decision Trees for Decision Making,"
HBR July-August 1964, p. 126,
or the more recent article by
Samuel E. Bodily,
"When Should You Go to Court?"
HBR May-June 1981, p. 103.

4 See David B. Hertz,
"Risk Analysis in Capital Investment,"
HBR January-February 1964, p. 95,
and John S. Hammond III,
"Better Decisions with Preference Theory,"
HBR November-December 1967, p. 123,
for descriptions of risk profiles
and utility functions, respectively.

5 Michael E. Porter,
Competitive Strategy
(New York: The Free Press, 1980),
pp. 299-357.

6 A comprehensive treatment of multi-
attribute utility analysis is provided by
Ralph L. Keeney and Howard Raiffa in
*Decisions with Multiple Objectives:
Preferences and Value Trade-offs*
(New York: Wiley, 1976).
Our example illustrates only the
basic ideas of the method and the sim-
plest form of analysis, linear and additive.

7 *The Art and Science of Negotiation*,
a forthcoming book by Howard Raiffa
(Cambridge: Belknap Press of
Harvard University Press)
will contain an extensive treatment
of this subject.
Jacob W. Ulvila's doctoral dissertation,
"Decisions with Multiple Objectives
in Integrative Bargaining"
(Harvard Business School, 1979),
also addresses this topic.

Terry W. Rothermel

Forecasting resurrected

*How forecasting can
gauge competitive
and market forces—
as far as
ten years out*

The use of forecasting in most companies is confined to short-term predictions, largely because top management is leery about the capabilities of economists and the reliability of their long-term calculations. But companies that treat modeling techniques as the stepchildren of strategic management may be overlooking an important management tool.

Here the author chronicles how forecasts in capital-intensive industries have proved remarkably accurate in predicting not only the most important variables of a particular market as long as ten years into the future but also the investment behavior of competitors as they react to the market. Such a high rate of success argues persuasively that forecasting could become the linchpin of competitive strategy for many companies. Using the technique requires management to correctly identify the strategic underpinnings of the competition's behavior. And that provides a better understanding of the company's own behavior—an important key to any successful strategy.

Mr. Rothermel is a member of the senior staff of Arthur D. Little, Inc. He has written numerous articles and lectures extensively on the use of forecasting models in industrial markets and on pollution control businesses. This is his first article for HBR.

The 1970s witnessed a decline in the respectability of forecasting and model building. That is not to say most companies don't forecast; in business planning there is no such thing as *not* forecasting. But companies concentrate on straightforward predictions of demand or sales based on historical and other verifiable data. Executives hold little faith in a corporate planner's ability to accurately predict anything else, partly because good forecasts, other than those of demand, are all too rare. Results are often made in such a tentative way—or the use of the forecast turns into such a disaster—that many would agree with Drucker's caustic premise that "forecasting is not a respectable human activity."

I won't argue that we can forecast everything. Certainly, I would agree that "no one pretends 'single events' can be predicted." But I do suggest that a sophisticated model-building approach can provide the sound base of information needed for competitive investment strategy.

I will discuss my nearly ten years of success with an industrial simulation technique. Typically a company in a capital-intensive industry uses it to forecast price and supply. This technique has proved to be an invaluable tool that allows the company to anticipate market forces and thus to forge a better strategic framework for competitive decision making.

What is its secret of success? This model teaches a company as much about its competition as it does about its market position. The reason is that this model-building technique requires the company to identify the underlying factors that guide the decisions of competitors. To do that, the model does not assume that the competition behaves in a rational manner; it would not work if it did. In fact, it forecasts correctly only when competitors are assumed to behave in simple Pavlovian fashion, responding to outside stimuli without sufficient thought as to the consequences.

In short, investment decisions of competing companies respond in phase, predicated more on current profits than on thoughtful estimates of tomorrow's returns. Price actions by one company are met by price overreaction by the competition, all at the expense of industrywide profitability.

Using this simulation teaches the company that success lies not in Pavlovian responses but in knowing and anticipating the competition and perhaps in making courageous countercyclical investment decisions that influence tomorrow's prices.

Companies also learn to look farther ahead at the impact of their own—and the competition's—market decisions. They begin to evaluate expansions of industrial capacity by competitors in light of the competitive dynamics of the industry. And, most important, they find that the timing of investment can and will determine success or failure.

I must declare that such models are never really completed or perfected; the learning process continues. Simulations evolve as they are integrated into strategic processes and as the estimates of the tangible and intangible variables are refined. Some variables may be kept and others tossed out altogether. After all, knowledge about the market grows, even as the marketplace itself changes. Although worshippers at the altar of hard data may point to these caveats as reason enough to reject the technique, the caveats do nothing to undermine the usefulness of the model.

If the profits of a company in a capital-intensive industry are buffeted by the storms of investment cycles, and if the company is committed to remaining in business, then an industrial market simulation is the most effective pilot plant for testing investment strategy.

Building the simulation

Think of these forecasting models as building blocks balanced on top of one another (see *Exhibit I*), each representing a sector of a typical industrial simulation. First are the twin blocks of demand and production-cost-profits, built on traditional data sources. The competitive materials and investment sectors come next, built on management experience. The market share and price sectors depend most directly on the investment and competitive materials sectors. All of these blocks support the desired result: improved competitive strategy.

The model sectors are not separate; they interact. The diagram gives a glimpse of the model's complexity—a simulation of the complexities of a real industrial market. Those looking for sure, easy

answers often underestimate the enormous task of successful forecasting. Good forecasting results cannot be had (with lower risks and costs) in a simple, stepwise fashion by working out a much simpler model, proving its usefulness, and gradually embellishing it until a complex system is reached. (For a description of the fusion of management experience into a model see the accompanying ruled insert.)

This simple approach misses the point of industry simulation experience and runs the risk of overlooking essential ingredients, leading to eventual failure and dissatisfaction. The danger in undertaking a full industry simulation, of course, is that overly complex models are often left unfinished. But the technique has surprised both forecasters and corporate executives by its power to chart an industry's course—a capability heretofore not found in simpler techniques and one all too rare in business planning practice.

The first steps

It is not necessary to reconstruct the entire learning process here. But a look at some sectors of the model may help you to understand how the technique has evolved and why it is an important tool. These models generally use traditional macroeconomic indexes and correlations to forecast demand. The demand sector is the easiest to construct since it is tied to verifiable data.

At this stage the most important lesson a company learns is that a test of alternative demand futures (using typical "what if" variations) requires a simulation of customer decisions relative to competitive materials substitution and price elasticity. For example, different materials compete for use in automobiles, different fuels in energy markets.

To take this into account, simulations add a competitive materials sector to the traditional forecast of demand, one that acknowledges a competitive presence outside the industry under study. The result: the impact of demand elasticity is greatest at the peaks and valleys of price and industry cycles. If such impact (which might be called the "relief valves of elasticity") is excluded, forecasts of supply imbalances can be misleading in supply-short or overcapacity situations.

The production-cost-profits sector is just as easy to forecast as demand because business managers of course monitor production and other costs before making industrial pricing decisions. Most corporate engineering departments know how to project investment requirements and the costs of production. So we factor in their intuition about competitors' costs. In addition, we find that we need to build in assumptions about plant "de-bottlenecking." How

| Exhibit I | **The building blocks of a typical industry simulation** |

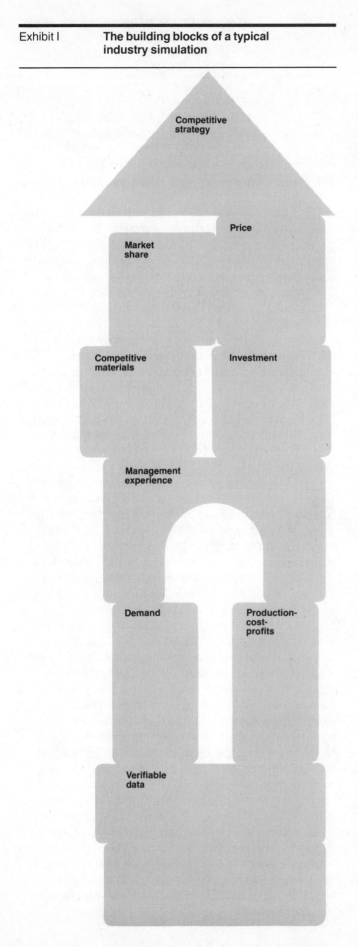

much more capacity will be available when the system is fully de-bottlenecked? How long will the de-bottlenecking take under conditions of short supply? How will it affect production costs over time? And will competitors behave differently?

While much business literature discusses the importance of market share to business success, precious little deals with the quantitative determinants of this share. The key remains that mysterious "invisible hand" that guides the market system toward equilibrium, seeking price relief for excesses of capacity or demand.

But simulation truly pays off in the market share sector; it teaches us that the hand may be less mysterious than we think. Lacking practical general algorithms, the simulator devises ad hoc mechanisms to produce realistic behavior and stand in for the unknown mechanism of the hand. For example, investment decisions (and resulting capacity shares) heavily affect market shares. Competitive actions of price, promotion, and product can have dramatic short-term effects on market share, and the imposition of a longer-term effect of capacity share helps reproduce realistic market share behavior for industrial markets.

The heart of the matter

A corporate economist I know once exclaimed, "Now I understand the secret to forecasting price – it lies in forecasting supply!" Supply forecasting *is* at the heart of these industry simulations and supply forecasting *is* their secret to price forecasting. But it is also the most neglected part of the economic triad of demand, supply, and price – the orphaned child of economic research. The supply sectors of these industry models prove to be the triggers of industrial supply, price, and profit cycles.

The springboard: price

The price forecasts produced by an industry simulation for two grades of a plastic material are indicated by the solid black lines in *Exhibit II.* We produced these five-year forecasts at time zero by an industry simulation, without benefit of subsequent improvements to the model and its inputs. The forecast captures the eventual trends in price and some, but obviously not all, of the break points. A shortage in "available" capacity led to a rise in the price for the lower-grade material during the first year – a rise that

Exhibit II	Comparison of forecast and actual prices for a plastic compound

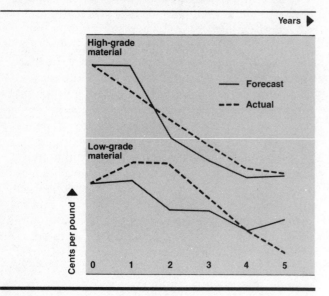

the model did not anticipate. Why? It was based on management's knowledge of significant entry of new capacity.

Ordinarily such capacity would lead to a price decline in both grades, but these particular facilities were expansions that required the temporary shutdown of plants in order to integrate shared operations. The excess capacity led instead to a temporary shortfall in supply at a time when overproduction normally would have resulted. Hence the price rise. Despite this problem, the price forecasts by this early, first-generation model proved to be powerful predictors of the timing and direction of price turns. And the model was a good intermediate-term forecasting tool.

Another lesson concerns the price "route." Most price forecasts postulate a linear movement over time, but that hardly ever happens. In *Exhibit III* a management team bringing in new capacity at the first point could see dramatically different profit results over time. If this capacity overloads the market circuits, downward pressure could be exerted on price to the detriment of profits. (Such a down-and-under scenario could be cause for early management retirements.)

Finally, the price forecasting models gave important insights into the time-honored theory of market equilibrium. In economic theory, price is anchored to the intersection of demand and supply curves—and to the concept of market equilibrium. Through these simulations, you learn that the forces of market equilibrium are at work, but they operate in a fluid, not a steady, state. The market reaches *toward* equilibrium; the problem is that once it gets there, it passes right on through to a new imbalance.

The capacity cycle forecast

Coincident with the limited success of its price forecasts, the simulation produced a more impressive industry forecast. I show a summary of an industry forecast for a plastics compound in *Exhibit IV*; it corresponds to the price forecasts shown in *Exhibit III*. Despite the unforeseen effects of the early entry of new capacity, the model proved its prescience for ten years by anticipating every major move in this product-industry cycle. I have graphically depicted this success by comparing the forecast variables with reality as reported by trade papers (represented by headlines taken from *Chemical Week* and *Chemical and Engineering News* and listed above the graph at various times).

The genesis of the industry cycle is found in a "grand loop" of logical reactions to industry conditions. The forecast industrywide operating rate (as a percentage of capacity) is represented on the upper line. Price forecasts (cents per pound) are on the middle line; supply is represented by the rate of entry of capacity (e.g., units of capacity per year) into the industry. (Note that this indicates incremental new, not cumulative, capacity.)

I'll first review the forecast scenario. In its first year, operating rates were high. Prices were to be stable (after a rise just before "takeoff") and profits were to be quite good. Under those conditions, the simulation indicated that producers would commit to expansions coming on stream two or three years later.

A key assumption built into the forecast was that capacity expansion by several producers in the second and third year would more than cover any increased demand. In response, operating rates would fall precipitously, and producers would use price to increase sales and market share. Price actions would trigger price reactions from competitors. The behavioral logic of the model then predicted that industry participants would sour on the business. (You can just imagine how the pleas for price statesmanship would appear in the press, as no one would admit to thoughts of future investment. Proclamations would ring out that the industry has learned its lesson and the cycle will not happen again!)

Meanwhile, operating rates would improve again with increased demand, partly stimulated by the lower prices. There would be a fall-off in the addition of new—and even some shutdowns of less economic—capacity. By the fifth year, operating rates would return to the high level of the first year; profit would improve but little new capacity would be on the horizon.

Exhibit III **The profit differences between two price points**

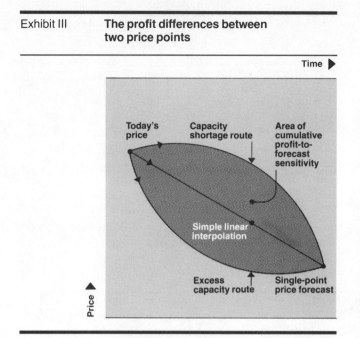

Time ▶

Today's price

Capacity shortage route

Area of cumulative profit-to-forecast sensitivity

Simple linear interpolation

Excess capacity route

Single-point price forecast

Price ▲

At this point, the model projected that the grand loop would begin again. Producers would put on their optimistic glasses, rose-tinted by higher operating rates, prices, and profits. The result would be a round of investments in new capacity coming on stream in the seventh year. That capacity expansion cycle would ultimately depress operating rates again, along with prices and investment attitudes.

How did it compare with reality?

The commentaries across the top of *Exhibit IV* are actual trade-press headlines. The model's power is shown by the uncanny parallel of its forecasts with events over a 12-year period. After five years, the model's validity already exceeded expectations. Given its success ten years out, we now assume that it benefits from more than just a little good fortune.

Mothballing of capacity in the real world coincided with the predicted bottoming out of prices in year 4. The headlines reveal that new capacity came on stream just as predicted in years 6-7 and 10-11 after successsive price recovery periods.

We found the model to be most powerful in calling the capacity expansion cycles underlying its price forecasts, despite the excess of demand over what was assumed as inputs. This difference did not seem to change the investment pattern at all. Without knowledge of the real future of demand, the original forecast still anticipated the actual timing of capacity expansion cycles – clearly suggesting a constancy (and a predictability) in industry investment behavior.

The economics of competition

Companies in capital-intensive industries should recognize this grand loop of excess capacity and capacity shortages. All too quickly decisions seem to feed on themselves, and delays only aggravate the problem. For example, the most important delay in the plastics example is the two or three years' lag between the investment commitment and the availability of new production capacity. The conditions that originally stimulated the decision may have disappeared (if not reversed themselves) in the interim.

The picture the models draw about the state of competitive decision making is not complimentary. Investments by competitors are made in response to the same business stimuli. Current profits are given more importance than studied estimates of tomorrow's likely returns on investment decisions. Price actions tend to be met by price reactions in an effort to seek or preserve market share, possibly at the expense of industrywide profitability. Responses to demand elasticities, in turn, do not reward price cuts as quickly as market share elasticities do.

The grand loop results from producers competing for the same block of increased demand, for the same apparent need for new capacity, for the same elasticity rewards of lower prices, and for the same comfort in making a cyclical decision.

The most important variables in this self-perpetuating industry cycle are human attitudes, incomplete information, and strategic mistakes – all of which receive only grudging acknowledgment in most economic theory. These industry simulations buttress the basic idea of "competitive economics" – that the corporation should focus more attention on competitive frontiers, on the "economics of the other guy."

Simulation helps prove that: (1) competitive economics are condition driven, (2) the "what is" dominates the "what should be," and (3) conditions in the marketplace severely limit the freedom of competitive decision making without diminishing the importance of the decisions that remain. Decisions are driven by financial objectives and economic law but modified by corporate ambition, imperfect knowledge, and management error.

Capacity gaps & the shadow forecast

In such simulation, a company tries to look inside the heads of its competitors as they make

Exhibit IV   **Forecast of an industry cycle for a plastic compound compared with actual trade-press headlines**

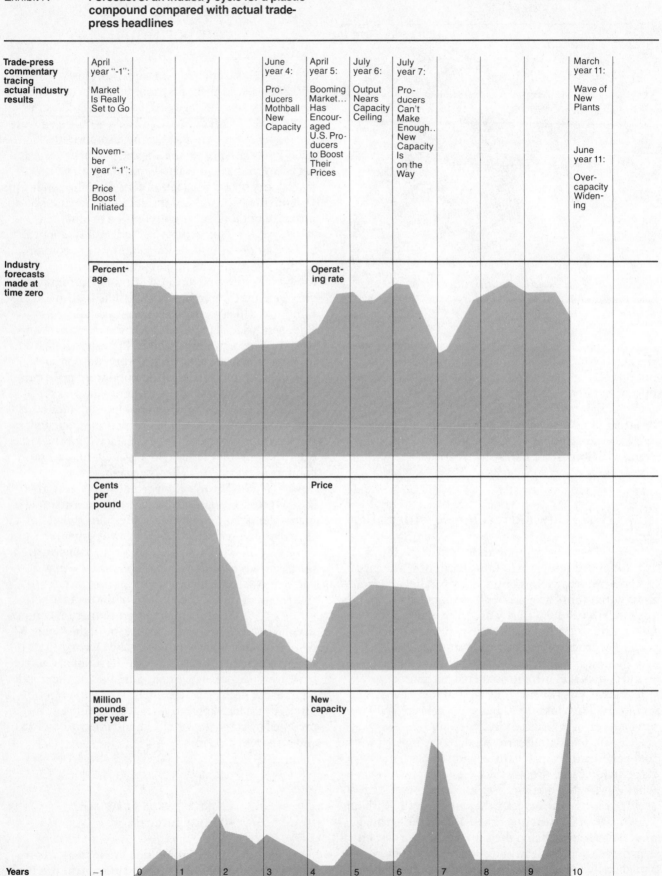

Trade-press commentary tracing actual industry results

April year "-1":

Market Is Really Set to Go

November year "-1":

Price Boost Initiated

June year 4:

Producers Mothball New Capacity

April year 5:

Booming Market... Has Encouraged U.S. Producers to Boost Their Prices

July year 6:

Output Nears Capacity Ceiling

July year 7:

Producers Can't Make Enough... New Capacity Is on the Way

March year 11:

Wave of New Plants

June year 11:

Overcapacity Widening

Industry forecasts made at time zero

Percentage

Operating rate

Cents per pound

Price

Million pounds per year

New capacity

Years   −1   0   1   2   3   4   5   6   7   8   9   10

their forecasts. Such an insight is called a "shadow forecast." Also in the jargon of industry simulation, we postulate that competitors continually search for "capacity gaps"; these are shortages that arise when capacity does not meet the demands of the market, which the competition then seeks to exploit with more investment.

We reflect the forecasting practices of competitors within the model as shadow forecasts, from the angles of both supply and demand. To do so we assume that competitors lack access to perfect information in the marketplace. By the time market facts turn from rumor into report, they have lost much of their value in giving competitive information. Of course, misleading shadow forecasts of demand can lead to significant investment-decision errors. For example, a competitor could misinterpret elasticity responses of demand to price changes as a general trend in demand. Or a competitor could read changes in market share as changes in demand. Both can prove false in the long run. The most misleading assumption a competitor may make is that market share will remain unchanged.

So when adding estimates of competitive capacities and expansion plans into our own forecast, we allow for a time lag. Delays in the availability of information alter the whole industry picture. Simultaneous decisions by competitors to invest in similar amounts of new capacity may not be known to each other until months later. At that point, it may be too late to alter psychological and business commitments. Competitors may then become even more aggressive in the pursuit of advance contracts.

We have learned that a competitor will blunder ahead. Each will react as if it were the only company in the market, i.e., once it identifies a capacity gap it will rush to fill in the whole gap, not the portion indicated by its share of the market. This will result in more capacity coming on stream than is necessary, with the subsequent impact on price and profit.

Investment behavior

Other competitive considerations in the model lead to some striking suggestions about the extremes between which different corporate investment decisions can swing. In the same industry, a new entrant and the market leader will view investment, and its possible results, in entirely different ways.

New competitors will make decisions on even less information than their established counterparts. In modeling the behavior of new entrants, we have usually assumed that an investment will be triggered when operating rates or profits reach a certain level. That may seem simplistic, too much of a knee-jerk reaction even for a novice company, but the resulting model behavior – achieving as it does such a remarkably close approximation of reality – persuades the analyst that when a new entrant begins to sell its product, it will be less concerned with high profits or a target market share than with survival and carving out some share for itself.

The decision process that we have observed in an industry simulation also suggests some refinements of traditional supply theories of economics. For example, we have found that price only indirectly creates supply. And that profits, perceptions of profits, or correlates of profits (like operating rates) may have a more direct impact on supply.

What makes an industry leader?

These industry simulations add fuel to the debate on leadership. Which company is the real leader in the market? How does its behavior affect others? What lessons can a competitor learn from the leader's actions?

This is one area where the model has not yet come up with a conclusive answer. If we look at the concept of a leader in terms of supply instead of price, we might expect such a company to act more rationally than anyone else – to invest at the right time and in the right-size plant. In practice, however, the supply leader may behave in the same way as the rest of industry – in fact, the leader may at times make the last and least-needed investment that eventually erodes operating rates, prices, and profits.

Actually, a true industry leader may buck the investment trend, avoid the crest of the investment wave, and bring new capacity on stream after that first wave has subsided.

This idea of countercyclical investment is attractive and may prove worthwhile. It seems to be a logical alternative to the more accepted form. As with any idea that lies outside common knowledge and experience, however, it carries more risk.

For example, if a producer hesitates to invest amidst a wave of industrial capacity expansions, he could be left behind and lose market share. The initial growth in industrywide capacity spurred by his competitors could far exceed expectations. So even when the wave crests and falls back, the industry could be left with excess volume. And when the producer that has held back finally brings a new plant on stream, he may find that his industry still suffers from too much capacity. Even taking into account these potential problems, however, such forecasting models may enable a company to focus its subsequent marketing

Five steps to a successful simulation

The first step, *conceptualization*, ensures the integration of management experience into the five basic model sectors or modules (demand, competitive materials, market share, production-cost-profits, investment, and price). Top management and the simulators discuss key ideas in a series of meetings. The simulators relate lessons learned in earlier industries and the elements common to each industry simulation; management responds by identifying its industry's special features.

It is up to management to describe variables in light of their perceived importance in the market. For example, in our simulation of a basic metals industry, key executives decided it was essential to simulate the end-use market as well. In a different way, a model for carpet fibers was designed to reflect up-to-date knowledge of the features of competitive fibers but did not simulate other industries in which all such fibers compete. The result of the first step is a series of preliminary flow diagrams.

The second stage, *functional design*, develops the modules prescribed in the first step: how decision rules will be formulated, how unknown relationships will be simulated, and how inputs will be defined. New functions need designing to fit the special character of the industry. For example, in the carpet simulation management wanted to integrate consumer perceptions. To influence market share, the simulators ended up using logarithmic values of the perceptions of different fibers. These first two stages are the most important and typically eat up more than 50% of the initial budget for the simulation.

In the next stage, *computerization*, programmers translate the designs of management and the simulators into a working model that processes inputs and develops outputs. Management then analyzes the results and decides whether they are too removed from reality. For instance, some of the original models produced results that did not reflect the real world. Management had characterized its competitors too rationally – as if they behaved in the way management hoped they would. Once more natural (irrational) behavior was factored in, the simulation really began to behave like the industry.

In the *debugging/fine tuning* stage, simulators work out the kinks and examine questionable results. They test the program for certain sensitivities (i.e., to a range of future demand alternatives) and then tune it to a range of other probable market events.

The final stage, *testing/updating*, is ongoing. As management begins to use the model as a tool, integrating it into the planning process, executives review various forecasts and further refine real-world inputs. Here the tool that has used management experiences in its development becomes a resource for management understanding.

efforts on particular product lines or product grades suffering from undercapacity.

More than any other form of investment, a company must carefully justify the countercyclical type, if only because it runs against intuition and common practice. Validity for any company depends on its financial resources, a careful financial analysis, a management concerned with long-term results (out at least five years), and confidence in this simulation technique – presumably from experience in comparing forecasts with results. Greater risk, of course, holds out the promise of greater reward.

From dialogue to decision

One view of forecasting has always struck me as particularly apt. In a paper presented to the 64th national meeting of the American Institute of Chemical Engineers, Albert Olenzak, director of corporate planning and economics at Sun Company, Inc., said, "Forecasting might be thought of as analogous to the illumination provided by the headlights of a car driving through a snowstorm at night. A bit of what lies ahead is revealed, not always clearly, so that the driver may find his way. It is not necessary for the driver to recognize every landmark and road sign, but merely to avoid danger and pick out enough detail so that he may arrive at his planned destination."

Simulation doesn't give all the answers. Sometimes it even seems to muddy the water, as with the industry leadership issue. But as an educational tool, it can provoke a meaningful dialogue through which managers can construct an important investment-decision framework.

Success in forecasting price and supply cycles depends on careful characterization and forecasting of the conditions surrounding a decision. Once they are established, a manager can foresee the likely direction and timing of competitors' decisions. To know the conditions of a decision is to know the decision.

These successful simulations of the conditions and the resulting decisions give testimony to the state of competitive investment strategy to date. Simply following the instincts of natural competitive behavior barely deserves the name strategy. More deserving would be a program based on understanding the competition, gauging capacity expansion cycles, and then timing investments accordingly.

A consequence of industry forecasting is the ability to anticipate trends. Calling the shots on an industry cycle allows decision makers to pick out the right spot for strategic action. When a company anticipates impending price actions, for example, it can consider price response beforehand. If the conditions seem right, a competitor's price cut can be quickly matched to avoid loss of contract or market share. If they are not right, a company can refuse to meet a price increase with the confidence that it is not likely to stick. Alternatively, a company can use the forecast as a basis for initiating price action in the market.

In the same way, we see how pricing decisions are determined by investment moves made earlier in an industry cycle. This relationship further suggests that the lifetime of an investment decision extends at least through the pricing decisions made before and after the new capacity enters the marketplace, i.e., today's investment decision is tomorrow's pricing decision. It is surprising that this supply-side determination of price is not more widely recognized in industry circles.

Industry simulation offers a strategic pilot plant for integrating investment decisions with the other major decisions of a business unit. Through sensitivity analysis, it can at least narrow the "envelope of uncertainty" of an industry's future. It is as useful to marketing and division managers as it is to strategic planners and corporate officers. Derivative competitive strategies range from strategic long-term investment decisions to short-term pricing tactics.

In short, it is a tool from which the whole company can benefit. It enables managers to formally use the "intangible" information on which good business judgment has always relied. Ultimately, it can lead to sharper thinking on the dynamics of a company's competitive position. ▽

Reprint 82209

How Royal Dutch/Shell developed a planning technique that teaches managers to think about an uncertain future

Scenarios: uncharted waters ahead

Pierre Wack

It is fashionable to downplay and even denigrate the usefulness of economic forecasting. The reason is obvious: forecasters seem to be more often wrong than right. Yet most U.S. companies continue to use a variety of forecasting techniques because no one has apparently developed a better way to deal with the future's economic uncertainty.

Still, there are exceptions, like Royal Dutch/Shell. Beginning in the late 1960s and early 1970s, Shell developed a technique known as "scenario planning." By listening to planners' analysis of the global business environment, Shell's management was prepared for the eventuality—if not the timing—of the 1973 oil crisis. And again in 1981, when other oil companies stockpiled reserves in the aftermath of the outbreak of the Iran-Iraq war, Shell sold off its excess before the glut became a reality and prices collapsed.

Undoubtedly, many readers believe they are familiar with scenarios. But the decision scenarios developed by Shell in Europe are a far cry from their usual U.S. counterparts. In this article and a sequel to come, the author describes their evolution and ultimate impact on Shell's management.

Mr. Wack is retired head of the business environment division of the Royal Dutch/Shell Group planning department, which he directed during the turbulent decade from 1971 to 1981. Wack, an economist, developed with Edward Newland the Shell system of scenario planning. He now consults and participates in scenario development with management teams around the world. In 1983 and 1984, he was senior lecturer in scenario planning at the Harvard Business School.

Illustration by Tom Briggs, Omnigraphics, Inc.

Few companies today would say they are happy with the way they plan for an increasingly fluid and turbulent business environment. Traditional planning was based on forecasts, which worked reasonably well in the relatively stable 1950s and 1960s. Since the early 1970s, however, forecasting errors have become more frequent and occasionally of dramatic and unprecedented magnitude.

Forecasts are not always wrong; more often than not, they can be reasonably accurate. And that is what makes them so dangerous. They are usually constructed on the assumption that tomorrow's world will be much like today's. They often work because the world does not always change. But sooner or later forecasts will fail when they are needed most: in anticipating major shifts in the business environment that make whole strategies obsolete (see the insert, "Wrong When It Hurts Most").

Most managers know from experience how inaccurate forecasts can be. On this point, there is probably a large consensus.

My thesis—on which agreement may be less general—is this: the way to solve this problem is not to look for better forecasts by perfecting techniques or hiring more or better forecasters. Too many forces work against the possibility of getting *the* right forecast. The future is no longer stable; it has become a moving target. No single "right" projection can be deduced from past behavior.

The better approach, I believe, is to accept uncertainty, try to understand it, and make it part of our reasoning. Uncertainty today is not just an occasional, temporary deviation from a reasonable predictability; it is a basic structural feature of the business environment. The method used to think about and plan for the future must be made appropriate to a changed business environment.

Royal Dutch/Shell believes that decision scenarios are such a method. As Shell's former

A note on names

Throughout this article, I use "Royal Dutch/Shell" and "Shell" to refer to the Royal Dutch/Shell group of companies. The terms also serve as a convenient shorthand to describe the management and planning functions within the central service companies of that group in London and The Hague. I am generally excluding Shell Oil Company of the United States, which – as a majority-owned public company – had undertaken its own operations planning. I use words like "company" as a shorthand for what is a complex group of organizations with varying degrees of self-sufficiency and operational independence. Most are obliged to plan for a future in their own national economic and political environments and to be integral parts of the Royal Dutch/Shell group of which they are members. I would not like to mislead anyone into thinking that any single person, manager, or planner is able to have a clear view of it all.

group managing director, André Bénard, commented: "Experience has taught us that the scenario technique is much more conducive to forcing people to think about the future than the forecasting techniques we formerly used."[1]

Many strategic planners may claim they know all about scenarios: they have tried but do not like them. I would respond to their skepticism with two points:

☐   Most scenarios merely quantify alternative outcomes of obvious uncertainties (for example, the price of oil may be $20 or $40 per barrel in 1995). Such scenarios are not helpful to decision makers. We call them "first-generation" scenarios. Shell's decision scenarios are quite different, as we shall see.

☐   Even good scenarios are not enough. To be effective, they must involve top and middle managers in understanding the changing business environment more intimately than they would in the traditional planning process. Scenarios help managers structure uncertainty when (1) they are based on a sound analysis of reality, and (2) they change the decision makers' assumptions about how the world works and compel them to reorganize their mental model of reality. This process entails much more than simply designing good scenarios. A willingness to face uncertainty and to understand the forces driving it requires an almost revolutionary transformation in a large organization. This transformation process is as important as the development of the scenarios themselves.

My discussion will be in two parts. In this first article I will describe the development of sce-

narios in the early 1970s as they evolved out of the more traditional planning process. As you will see, the concept and the technique we arrived at is very different from that with which we began – mainly because there were some highly instructive surprises along the way for all concerned. The art of scenarios is not mechanistic but organic; whatever we had learned after one step advanced us to the next.

In a forthcoming article, I will examine a short-term application of the technique and conclude by discussing key aspects that make the discipline creative.

The first steps

For ten years after World War II, Shell concentrated on physical planning: the company had to expand its production capacity and build tankers, depots, pipelines, and refineries. Its biggest challenge, like that of many companies, was to coordinate the scheduling of new facilities. Then from 1955 to 1965, financial considerations became more important but primarily on a project basis.

In 1965, Shell introduced a new system called "Unified Planning Machinery" (UPM) to provide planning details for the whole chain of activity – from moving oil from the ground, to the tanker, to the refinery, all the way to the gas station on the corner. UPM was a sophisticated, worldwide system that looked ahead six years: the first year in detail, the next five in broader lines. Unconsciously, managers designed the system to develop Shell's businesses in a familiar, predictable world of "more of the same."

Given the long lead times for new projects in an oil company, however, it was soon decided that the six-year horizon was too limited. Shell therefore undertook experimental studies to explore the business environment of the year 2000. One of them revealed that expansion simply could not continue and predicted that the oil market would switch from a buyers' to a sellers' market, with major discontinuities in the price of oil and changing interfuel competition. The study also signaled that major oil companies could become huge, heavily committed, and much less flexible – almost like dinosaurs. And dinosaurs, as we all know, did not adjust well to sudden environmental changes.

In view of the study's findings, Shell believed it had to find a new way to plan. It asked a dozen of its largest operating companies and business sectors

1 André Bénard,
"World Oil and Cold Reality,"
HBR November-December 1980, p. 91.

Wrong when it hurts most

In few fields has the concentration of the best techniques and the best brains been as high as that in short-term macroeconomic forecasting for the United States. Stephen McNees of the Federal Reserve Bank of Boston has been analyzing the track record of the best-known economic forecasters since 1970. For more than half of this period, they were quite successful. But on four occasions, the magnitude of error was large. McNees observes that:

"Forecasts made from 1973 through early 1974 initially did not foresee the recession and later misinterpreted the severe recession as an 'energy spasm.' "

"Forecasts made from mid-1977 through early 1978 did not capture the acceleration of the inflation rate in 1978 and 1979."

"Forecasts made during the 1980 recession underestimated the strength of the early recovery."

"Forecasts made in 1981 and early 1982 underestimated the severity of the 1982 recession and the deceleration of inflation that accompanied it."[1]

In the summer of 1981, the median one-year-ahead forecast of five prominent forecasters had predicted 2.1% growth in U.S. GNP for 1982. Instead, the economy plunged into a deep recession, with a GNP decline of 1.8%. As journalist Warren Brookes commented, "This is like forecasting partly cloudy and getting a ten-inch snowstorm instead. After all, in economics as in meteorology, it's the ability to predict stormy change that makes forecasting useful."

Many business cases illustrate a similar phenomenon. The oil industry—which before 1973 enjoyed the steadiest growth of all major industries—is still living with its failure to anticipate the turbulent changes that have occurred since then. Here is one major oil company's forecast of oil demand, made as late as 1978. This company allocates more resources to analyzing the future environment than do most companies and is well respected for its professionalism. Yet note how far outside the forecast demand range reality proved to be in 1984.

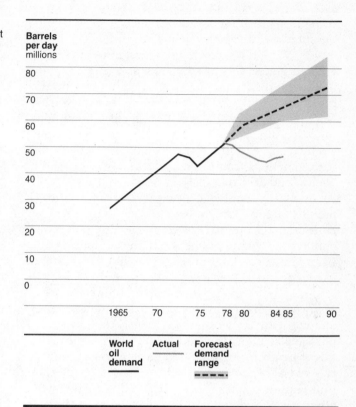

Barrels per day millions

World oil demand

Actual

Forecast demand range

1 Stephen K. McNees and John Ries, "The Track Record of Macroeconomic Forecasts," *New England Economic Review*, November-December 1983, p. 5.

to experiment and look ahead 15 years in an exercise called "Horizon Year Planning."

At the time, I worked for Shell Française. We were familiar with the late Herman Kahn's scenario approach and were intrigued by its possibilities for corporate planning.

Two important uncertainties made France a perfect testing ground for a corporate experiment with the technique: the availability of natural gas (then recently developed in France and the Netherlands), the only fuel that could compete with oil, and the political uncertainty surrounding the way France would manage energy. France's oil regime of that time favored national companies and severely limited Shell's market share.

But France, as a member of the European Community, might have had to change its oil regime at some point to conform to EC policy. The two options—no change or liberalization—combined with two alternatives, large or small availability of gas, gave us four potential scenarios, as illustrated in *Exhibit I*.

How far to go in describing each? We discovered quickly that we would almost quadruple our work load if we made each scenario as detailed as a normal plan under the UPM system. Just as the logistics of supply for an army have to be adapted to the type of war being fought, the logistics of scenario planning require a capacity to deal easily and quickly with alternatives. Without it, the whole process can be paralyzed by a bottleneck. In practice, this realization led later to our developing flexible simulation models and having a number of specialists in key areas who could rapidly assess the consequences of different alternatives.

More important, we realized that simply combining obvious uncertainties did not help much with decision making. That exercise brought us only to a set of obvious, simplistic, and conflicting strategic solutions. In fact, many companies are doing just that in their approach to scenarios—quantifying the obvious and not gaining any help in making decisions. Yet this negative realization led to discovery of a positive search tool. By carefully studying some uncertainties, we gained a deeper understanding of their interplay, which, paradoxically, led us to learn what was certain and inevitable and what was not.

We began to appreciate the importance of sorting out "predetermined elements" and "uncertainties" (see the insert, "What Is Predetermined and What Is Uncertain"). In emphasizing only uncertainties, and obvious ones at that, the scenarios we had developed were merely first-generation scenarios. They were useful in gaining a better understanding of the situation in order to ask better questions and develop better second-generation scenarios—that is, decision scenarios. This dawning intuition—confirmed by all later experience—was an awareness of the critical importance of

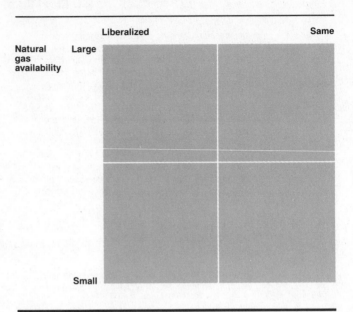

Exhibit I   **1970 scenarios**

design. Scenarios will either help decision makers or be of little use to them, depending on how they are constructed and presented, not just on the outcome they focus on. In the same way, two architects can create a well- or a poorly designed building, even though they both use the same construction materials.

The results of the horizon study across the company confirmed the conclusions of the year 2000 study. The most important findings were:

☐   The oil market—long characterized by oversupply—was due to switch to a sellers' market.

☐   Soon there would be virtually no spare crude oil supply capacity.

☐   Inevitably, the Middle East and, in particular, the Arabian Gulf would be the balancing source of oil supply.

☐   The great demand on Middle East production would bring a sharp reduction in the Middle East reserve-production ratio, if met.

☐   The sharp peak in Middle East production would not be allowed to occur. Intervening factors would include a desire by Arab countries to extend the lifetime of their one valuable resource and a cornering of the world energy market by Gulf producers for perhaps 10 to 15 years by limiting production.

☐   Only something approaching a sustained worldwide depression could reduce the growth of demand for Middle East oil to levels where the anticipated sellers' market would be too weak to command substantially higher oil prices.

The magnitude of the changes anticipated cast doubt on the ability of the UPM system to provide realistic planning assumptions. How could it provide the right answer if the forecasts on which it was based were likely to be wrong? In 1971, Shell therefore decided to try scenario planning as a potentially better framework for thinking about the future than forecasts—which were now perceived as a dangerous substitute for real thinking in times of uncertainty and potential discontinuity. But Shell, like many large organizations, is cautious. During the first year, when scenario analysis was done on an experimental basis, the company continued to employ the UPM system. In 1972, scenario planning was extended to central offices and certain large Shell national operating companies. In the following year, it was finally recommended throughout the group and UPM was then phased out.

The next step

The scenario process started with the construction of a set of exploratory first-generation scenarios. As we have learned, it is almost impossible to jump directly to proper decision scenarios.

☐ Scenario I was surprise-free, virtually lifted whole from the work done under the old UPM system. The surprise-free scenario is one that rarely comes to pass but, in my experience, is essential in the package. It builds on the implicit views of the future shared by most managers, making it possible for them to recognize their outlook in the scenario package. If the package only contains possibilities that appear alien to the participants, they will likely find the scenario process threatening and reject it out of hand.

☐ Scenario II postulated a tripling of host-government tax take in view of the 1975 renegotiation of the Teheran Agreement (which set the take for OPEC) and anticipated lower economic growth and depressed energy and oil demand as a consequence.

☐ Scenario III treated the other obvious uncertainty: low growth. Based on the 1970-1971 recession model, a proliferation of "me-first" values, and a growing emphasis on leisure, it assumed an economic growth rate only half of that projected under Scenario I, with a slowdown in international trade, economic nationalism, and protective tariffs. Low oil demand would limit oil price rises and lower producer government take.

☐ Scenario IV assumed increased demand for coal and nuclear energy—at the expense of oil.

All four scenarios assumed that the tax take of the producer governments would be increased at the 1975 Teheran renegotiation (see *Exhibit II*).

What is predetermined and what is uncertain

Strictly speaking, you can forecast the future only when all of its elements are predetermined. By predetermined elements, I mean those events that have already occurred (or that almost certainly will occur) but whose consequences have not yet unfolded.

Suppose, for example, heavy monsoon rains hit the upper part of the Ganges River basin. With little doubt you know that something extraordinary will happen within two days at Rishikesh at the foothills of the Himalayas; in Allahabad, three or four days later; and at Benares, two days after that. You derive that knowledge not from gazing into a crystal ball but from simply recognizing the future implications of a rainfall that has already occurred.

Identifying predetermined elements is fundamental to serious planning. You must be careful, however. Paul Valéry, the twentieth-century French philosopher, said, "Un fait mal observé est plus pernicieux qu'un mauvais raisonnement." (A fact poorly observed is more treacherous than faulty reasoning.) Errors in futures studies usually result from poor observation rather than poor reasoning.

There are always elements of the future that are predetermined. But there are seldom enough of them to permit a single-line forecast that encompasses residual uncertainties. Decision makers facing uncertain situations have a right to know just how uncertain they are. Accordingly, it is essential to try to put as much light on critical uncertainties as on the predetermined elements. They should not be swept under the carpet.

OK as numbers but—

This set of scenarios seemed reasonably well designed and would fit most definitions of what scenarios should be. It covered a wide span of possible futures, and each scenario was internally consistent.

When the set was presented to Shell's top management, the problem was the same as in the French scenarios: no strategic thinking or action could be taken from considering this material.

Many companies reach this same point in planning scenarios. Management reaction? "So what! What do I do with scenarios?" And planners abandon the effort, often because they believe the problem is, in part, management's inability to deal with uncertainty.

Yet this group of Shell managers was highly experienced in dealing with risk and uncertainty. For example, many of the decisions they make deal with exploratory drilling, a true uncertainty since you never know what you'll find until you drill. They must often decide whether to risk $5 million or $50

Exhibit II   **Producer government take***
1970-1985

Dollars per barrel

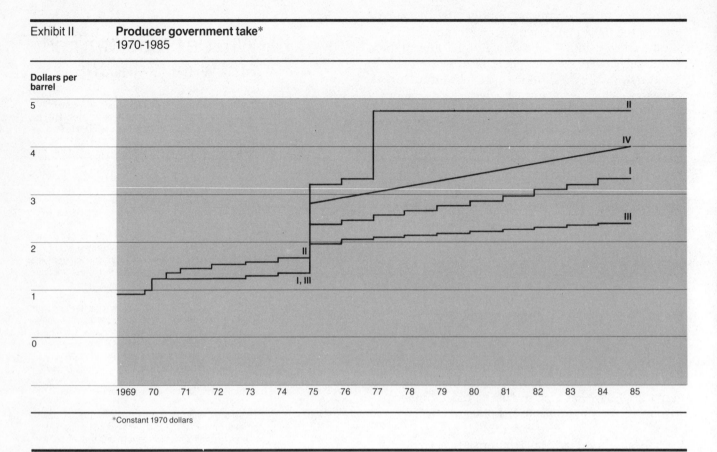

*Constant 1970 dollars

million on exploration projects and distinguish the risks, say, in Brazil or the North Sea. What was so different about the uncertainties of scenarios? Quite simply, they needed structuring. In oil exploration, there were theories to call on, concepts to use, an organized body of geological and geophysical analyses, comparisons with similar geological structures, and ways to spread the risk that were familiar to the decision maker. The first-generation scenarios presented the raw uncertainties but they offered no basis on which managers could exercise their judgment. Our next task was to provide that basis so that executives could understand the nature of these uncertainties and come to grips with them.

The goal of these exploratory first-generation scenarios is not action but understanding. Their purpose is to give insight into the system, to identify the predetermined elements, and to perceive connections among various forces and events driving the system. As the system's interrelatedness became clear, we realized that what may appear in some cases to be uncertain might actually be predetermined—that many outcomes were simply *not* possible.

These exploratory scenarios were not effective planning devices. Without them, however, we could not have developed the next generation of scenarios.

What will happen— what cannot

To understand the fluctuations that give the oil system its character and determine its future, we had to understand the forces that drive it. Work on the next set of scenarios began with a closer look at the principal actors in Shell's business environment: oil producers, consumers, and companies. Because self-interest determined the fundamental concerns of these groups, significant behavioral differences existed. So we began to study the characters on the stage and how they would behave as the drama unfolded.

In analyzing the major oil-producing countries one by one, for example, it was clear that Iran's interests differed from Saudi Arabia's or Nigeria's and that their strategies would reflect these differences. The lower panel of *Exhibit III* shows Iran's oil production as its share of projected oil demand under each of the 1971 scenarios, as well as discovery rates and additions to reserves. For the first five years, we expected that Iran's reserves would grow as the industry found more new oil than it would produce. For the second five years, we expected the situation to reverse and reserves to fall.

As the upper panel of *Exhibit III* shows, reserve-production ratios would drop rapidly under all

Exhibit III   Iran's production scenarios

Reserve/production ratios

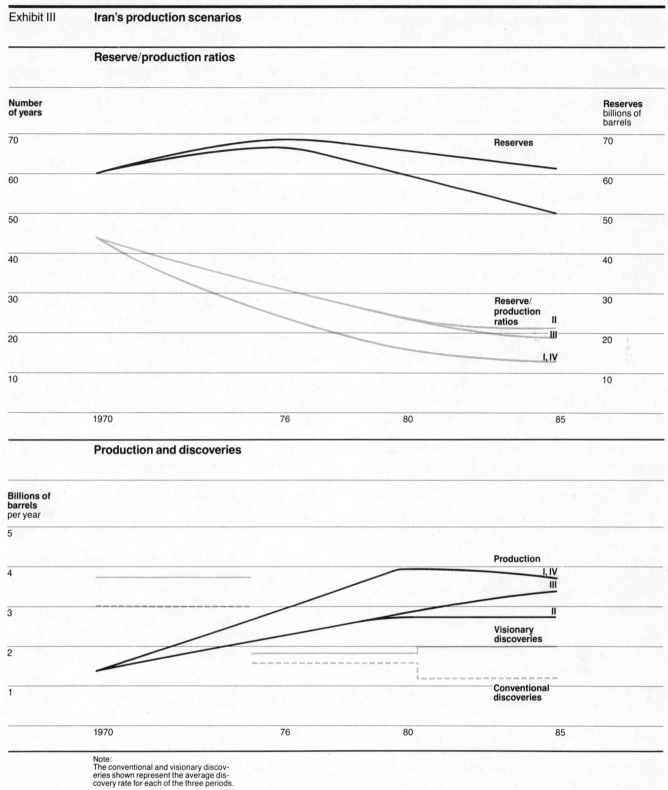

Note:
The conventional and visionary discoveries shown represent the average discovery rate for each of the three periods.

scenarios. Our conclusion was that Iran would then strive to change its oil policy from one of expanding production to one of increasing prices and possibly curbing production. Such a policy change would stem not from an anti-Western attitude but simply from the logic of national interest. If we were Iranian, we would behave the same way.

Saudi Arabia's situation was different. Except in the low-growth scenario, production would generate more revenue than the government could purposefully spend, even allowing for some "manageable" surplus. We concluded that even though oil company logic would have the Saudis producing 20 million barrels per day by 1985, the government could not do so in good political conscience. It was no surprise when Sheikh Zhaki Ahmed Yamani, Saudi Arabia's minister for oil affairs, later remarked: "We should find that leaving our crude in the ground is by far more profitable than depositing our money in the banks, particularly if we take into account the periodic devaluation of many of the currencies. This reassessment would lead us to adopt a production program that ensures that we get revenues which are only adequate for our real needs."[2]

We analyzed each of the producer countries according to their oil reserves and their need and ability to spend oil income productively (Exhibit IV). When arrayed in the simple matrix shown in Exhibit V, the power that was to become OPEC emerged clearly: no nation had both ample reserves and ample absorptive capacity, that is, the motivation to produce these reserves. If Indonesia, with its large population and enormous need for funds, had Saudi Arabia's reserves, then the growth of demand foreseen under the first scenario might have developed. But such was not the case.

We then analyzed the oil-consuming countries and saw their annual increments in import requirements (see Exhibit VI). For many years, oil imports had increased at a rate of about one million barrels per day; then for a long time the rate was about two million barrels per day.

Suddenly, in the mid-1970s, oil imports were expected to increase annually at much higher rates. This change can be understood by looking at Exhibit VII, which shows the sources of energy supply in the United States, Western Europe, and Japan. In the United States, oil supply had peaked early, and the incremental demand for energy had been satisfied by natural gas. Because of its regulated price, however, natural gas production plateaued in 1972. Coal production might have increased, but in light of the forecasts of future nuclear power generation, coal resources were not being developed. Nuclear plants, however, were not functioning in sufficient numbers to meet the demand, which was increasing annually at a rapid pace. Since the base was so large to begin with, even a 3% or 4%

increase in the U.S. energy demand would in turn demand a great deal of the only available incremental energy source—imported oil.

In Japan—then like a new continent emerging on the world economic map—circumstances were different. In 1953, as the U.S. occupation ended, Japanese industrial production was 40% of the United Kingdom's; in 1970, it was more than double. With the economy growing by 11% or 12% a year, annual demand for oil increased by some 20%. The result: huge increases in oil imports.

Beyond the need to view each participant individually and as part of a group, we discovered that "soft" data were as important to us as "hard" data in analyzing outcomes. For example, because the Japanese become anxious when faced with a possible denial of imports, any tension over oil supply would be especially trying. Furthermore, they would project on multinational oil companies the type of behavior they expect from their own companies in a crisis: giving loyalty to the home country and ignoring the rest of the world. This attitude would add to the probable tension over oil supplies.

Having collected and analyzed hard and soft data, and in order to expand the number of predetermined elements and get at the core of what remained uncertain, we looked at:

Oil demand by market class and at different rates of growth.

The implications of high oil prices for each nation's balance of payments and inflation.

The possible reactions of consumer governments to higher oil prices.

Interfuel competition and the impact of higher oil prices.

The changing "cut of the barrel."

Construction of refinery, marine, and market facilities.

2 Quoted in Platt's Oilgram,
February 10, 1972.

Exhibit IV How oil producers were motivated

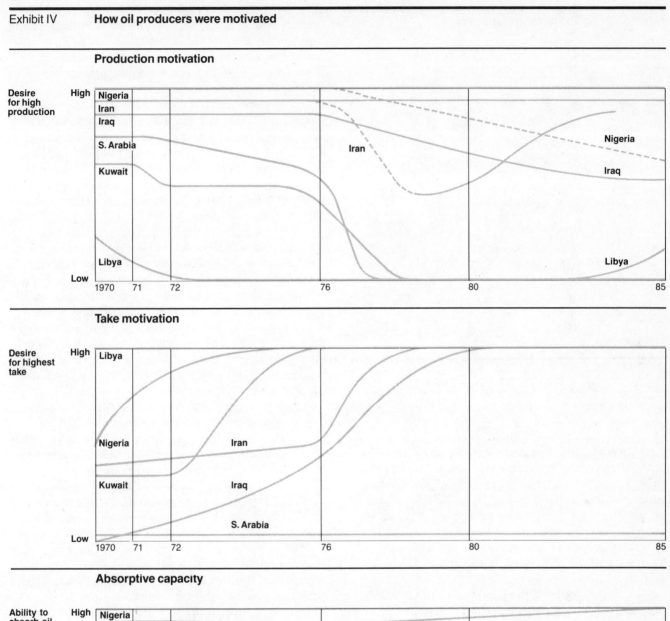

Production motivation

Desire
for high
production

High
Nigeria
Iran
Iraq
S. Arabia
Kuwait
Libya
Low

1970 71 72 76 80 85

Nigeria
Iran
Iraq
Libya

Take motivation

Desire
for highest
take

High
Libya
Nigeria
Kuwait
Iran
Iraq
S. Arabia
Low

1970 71 72 76 80 85

Absorptive capacity

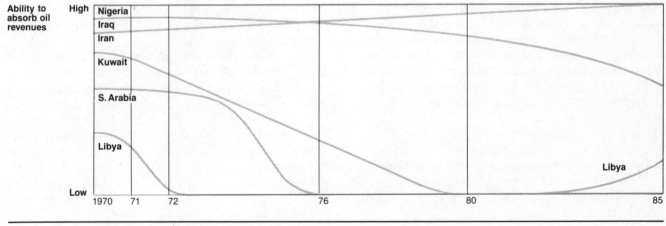

Ability to
absorb oil
revenues

High
Nigeria
Iraq
Iran
Kuwait
S. Arabia
Libya
Low

1970 71 72 76 80 85

Libya

Note:
The dotted lines show how a low take
would affect Iran's production motivation
and how low discoveries would affect
Nigeria's production motivation.

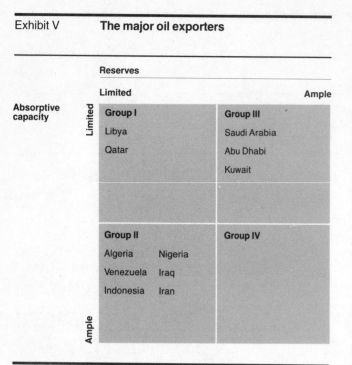

Exhibit V   **The major oil exporters**

Absorptive capacity	Reserves	
	Limited	Ample
Limited	**Group I** Libya Qatar	**Group III** Saudi Arabia Abu Dhabi Kuwait
Ample	**Group II** Algeria Nigeria Venezuela Iraq Indonesia Iran	**Group IV**

The 1972 scenarios

Having all these building blocks, we could begin to understand the forces driving the system. In response, we presented the revamped scenarios to Shell's top management as an array of possible futures, gathered in two families, A and B, in September 1972.* The A-group timed an oil supply disruption to coincide with the scheduled renegotiation of the Teheran price agreement in 1975. (In reality, it came, of course, in the fall of 1973 – after the imposition of the oil embargo.)

Most oil-producing countries would be reaching the technical limit of their capacities by 1976, while others would be reluctant to increase output further because of their inability to absorb the additional revenues. Accordingly, producer countries' oil prices would increase substantially by the end of 1975. Confronted with possible energy supply shortages and increased oil import bills, consuming countries would feel economic shock waves.

Because we had identified a predetermined element, we used the A-family of scenarios to examine three potential solutions to the problems it presented: private enterprise (A1); government intervention, or *dirigiste* (A2); or none (A3), resulting in an energy crisis.

*Author's note: With hindsight, this set of scenarios was still clumsily designed. Six are far too many; they had no proper names to convey the essence of what drives each scenario. The sequel to this article will include a discussion of design.

The A-family of scenarios emerged as the most likely outcome, but it varied sharply from the implicit worldview then prevailing at Shell. That view can be characterized loosely as "explore and drill, build refineries, order tankers, and expand markets." Because it was so different, how could our view be heard? In response, we created a set of "challenge scenarios," the B-family. Here the basic premise was that somehow, a sufficient energy supply would be available. The B-family scenarios would not only challenge the assumptions underlying the A-family but also destroy many of the business-as-usual aspects of the worldview held by so many at Shell (like their counterparts in other companies).

Under the B1 scenario, for example, some ten years of low economic growth were required to fit demand to the oil supply presumed available. While such low growth seemed plausible in the 1971 downturn, by 1972 signs of a coming economic boom began to show. B1 was also implausible since governments and citizens of industrialized countries viewed rising unemployment as unacceptable and would consciously seek growth no matter what. The implausibilities under B1 made the inevitability of a major disruption more plain to managers.

B3 was also an important educational tool because it postulated a very high supply of oil as a way to avoid major change. We called it the "three-miracles" scenario because it required the simultaneous occurrence of three extremely unlikely situations. The first was a miracle in exploration and production. The Shell exploration and production staff estimated a 30% chance that the reserves necessary to meet 1985 demand would be found in each of the oil provinces individually, but only a very small chance that these high reserves would be found in all areas simultaneously. Meeting the forecast 1985 demand under B3 would require not only 24 million barrels daily from Saudi Arabia, but also 13 million barrels from Africa and 6 million barrels from Alaska and Canada – clearly an impossibility.

The second miracle was sociopolitical: B3 foresaw that all major producing countries would happily deplete their resources at the will of the consumer. Countries with low capacities to absorb the excess revenue would agree to produce huge amounts of oil and put their money in the bank, exposed to the erosion of inflation, rather than keep it in the ground. That miracle projected the values of consuming countries onto oil producers – a kind of Western cultural imperialism that was extremely unconvincing, even to the most expansion-minded manager.

The final miracle started with the recognition that no capacity would be left above projected demand. Previously, when minor crises developed, additional oil was always available to meet sudden short-term needs. Under B3, however, there would be no

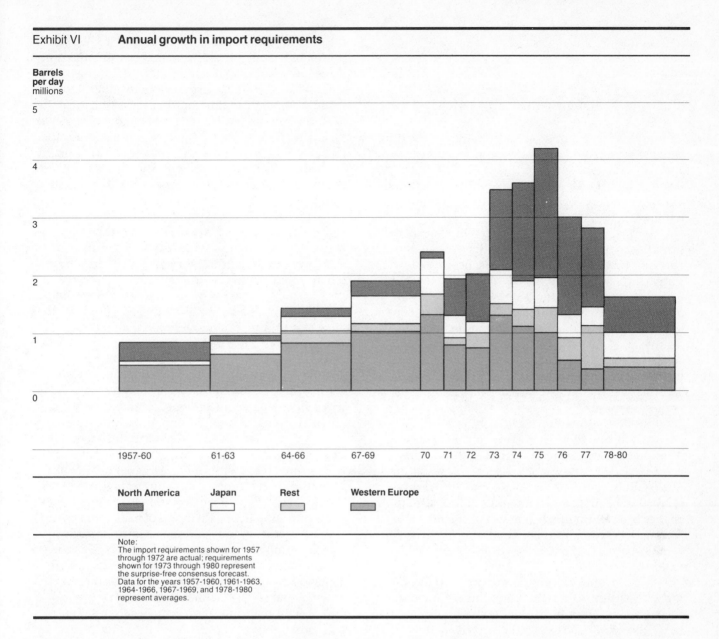

Exhibit VI   **Annual growth in import requirements**

Barrels per day millions

North America   Japan   Rest   Western Europe

Note:
The import requirements shown for 1957
through 1972 are actual; requirements
shown for 1973 through 1980 represent
the surprise-free consensus forecast.
Data for the years 1957-1960, 1961-1963,
1964-1966, 1967-1969, and 1978-1980
represent averages.

spare production capacity. The miracle then was that there would be no need for it – no wars in the region, no acts of God, no cyclical peaks of demand higher than anticipated. Again, this was nothing short of miraculous. The improbability of B3 forced Shell management to realize how disruptive the change in their world would be.

B2 was a totally artificial construct. It premised that – despite all the problems – the world would muddle through. This reflects the sentiment that, as William Ogburn said, "There is much stability in society....Social trends seldom change their directions quickly and sharply....Revolutions are rare and evolution is the rule." We couldn't rationally justify this scenario, but we realized that the worst outcome does not always develop. So we imagined a B2 scenario in which everything positive was possible. Oil

producers would live and let live to obtain concessions from the consumers who, in turn and with great foresight, would immediately curb oil consumption.

We quantified both the A- and B-family scenarios in terms of volume, price, impact on individual oil producers and consumers, and interfuel competition. Our presentation gained the attention of top management principally because the B-family of scenarios destroyed the ground many of them had chosen to stand on. Management then made two decisions: to use scenario planning in the central offices and the larger operating companies and to informally advise governments of the major oil-consuming countries about what we saw coming.

We made a series of presentations to the governments of the major consuming countries and stressed the coming disruption by tracing its impact on their balance of payments, rates of inflation, and resource allocation.

Banging the drum quickly

Shell first asked its major downstream operating companies to evaluate current strategies against two A-type scenarios, using the B2 scenario as a sensitivity check. By asking "what if," the B2 checked strategies already conceived in another conceptual framework (the A-family).

To this intent, we presented the A and B scenarios to the second echelon of Shell's management – its first exposure to scenarios. The meetings stood in stark contrast to traditional UPM planning sessions, which dealt out forecasts, trends, and premises – all under an avalanche of numbers. The scenarios focused less on predicting outcomes and more on understanding the forces that would eventually compel an outcome; less on figures and more on insight. The meetings were unusually lengthy and the audience clearly appreciative. We thought we had won over a large share of these managers.

The following months would show, however, that no more than a third of Shell's critical decision centers were really acting on the insights gained through the scenarios and actively preparing for the A-family of outcomes. The scenario package had sparked some intellectual interest but had failed to change behavior in much of the Shell organization. This reaction came as a shock and compelled us to rethink how to design scenarios geared for decision making.

Reality was painful: most studies dealing with the future business environment, including these first scenarios, have a low "existential effectiveness." (We can define existential effectiveness as single-mindedness, but the Japanese express it much better: "When there is no break, not even the thickness of a hair, between a man's vision and his action.") A vacuum cleaner is mostly heat and noise; its actual effectiveness is only around 40%. Studies of the future, particularly when they point to an economic disruption, are less effective than a vacuum cleaner.

If your role is to be a corporate lookout and you clearly see a discontinuity on the horizon, you had better learn what makes the difference between a more or a less effective study. One of the differences involves the basic psychology of decision making.

Every manager has a mental model of the world in which he or she acts based on experience and knowledge. When a manager must make a decision, he or she thinks of behavior alternatives within this mental model. When a decision is good, others will say the manager has good judgment. In fact, what

has really happened is that his or her mental map matches the fundamentals of the real world. We call this mental model the decision maker's "microcosm"; the real world is the "macrocosm."

There is also a corporate view of the world, a corporate microcosm. During a sabbatical year in Japan, for example, I found that Nippon Steel did not "see" the steel market in the same way as Usinor, the French steel giant. As a result, there were marked differences in the behavior and priorities of the two corporations. Each acted rationally, given its worldview. A company's perception of its business environment is as important as its investment infrastructure because its strategy comes from this perception. I cannot overemphasize this point: unless the corporate microcosm changes, managerial behavior will not change; the internal compass must be recalibrated.

From the moment of this realization, we no longer saw our task as producing a documented view of the future business environment five or ten years ahead. Our real target was the microcosms of our decision makers: unless we influenced the mental image, the picture of reality held by critical decision makers, our scenarios would be like water on a stone. This was a different and much more demanding task than producing a relevant scenario package.

We had first tried to produce scenarios that we would not be ashamed of when we subsequently compared them with reality. After our initiation with these first sets of scenarios, we changed our goal. We now wanted to design scenarios so that managers would question their own model of reality and change it when necessary, so as to come up with strategic insights beyond their minds' previous reach. This change in perspective – from producing a "good" document to changing the image of reality in the heads of critical decision makers – is as fundamental as that experienced when an organization switches from selling to marketing.

The 1973 scenarios – the rapids

More than 20 centuries ago, Cicero noted, "It was ordained at the beginning of the world that certain signs should prefigure certain events." As we prepared the 1973 scenarios, all economic signs pointed to a major disruption in oil supply. New analyses foretold a tight supply-demand relationship in the coming years.

Now we saw the discontinuity as predetermined. No matter what happened in particular, prices would rise rapidly in the 1970s, and oil produc-

Exhibit VII **Energy demand by sources**

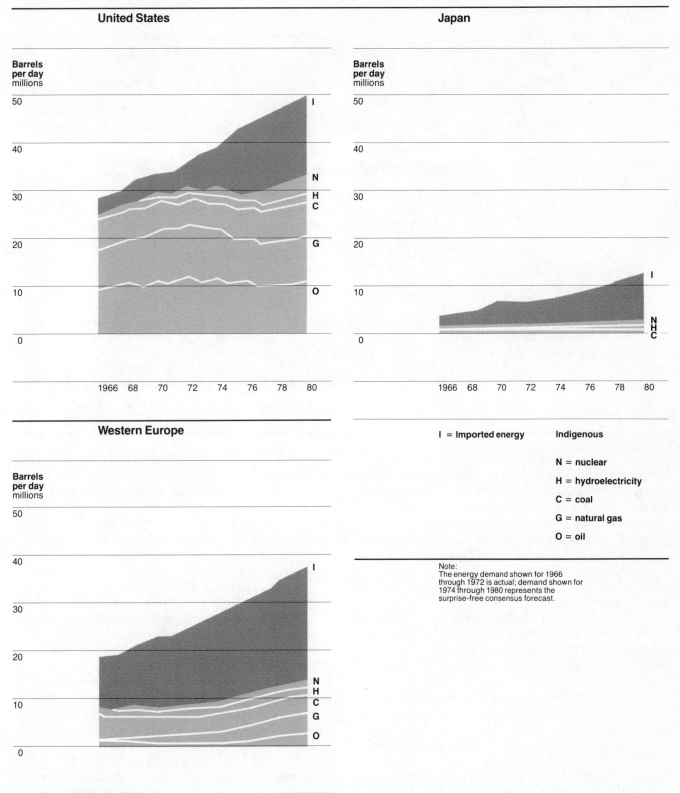

United States

Japan

Western Europe

I = Imported energy   Indigenous

N = nuclear

H = hydroelectricity

C = coal

G = natural gas

O = oil

Note:
The energy demand shown for 1966
through 1972 is actual; demand shown for
1974 through 1980 represents the
surprise-free consensus forecast.

Exhibit VIII   **1973 scenarios**

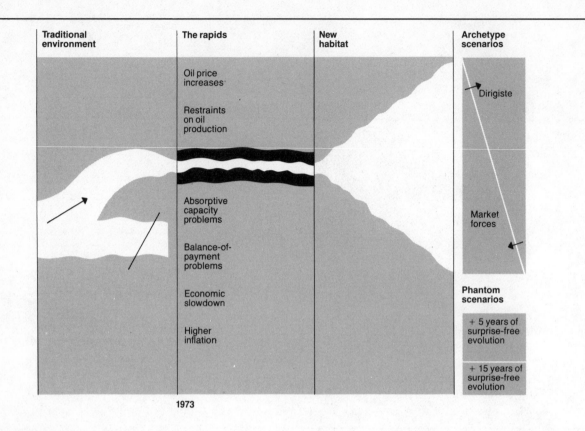

Traditional environment

The rapids
- Oil price increases
- Restraints on oil production
- Absorptive capacity problems
- Balance-of-payment problems
- Economic slowdown
- Higher inflation

New habitat

Archetype scenarios
- Dirigiste
- Market forces

Phantom scenarios
- + 5 years of surprise-free evolution
- + 15 years of surprise-free evolution

1973

tion would be constrained—not because of a real shortage of oil but for political reasons, with producers taking advantage of the very tight supply-demand relationship. Our next step was to make the disruption into our surprise-free scenario. We did not know how soon it would occur, how high the price increase would be, and how the various players would react. But we knew it would happen. Shell was like a canoeist who hears white water around the bend and must prepare to negotiate the rapids.

To help reframe our managers' outlook, we charted the 1973 scenarios (*Exhibit VIII*). From the calm upriver of the traditional environment, the company would plunge into the turbulence of the rapids and have to learn to live in a new habitat.

We could eliminate some of the original scenarios. We could dam off the alternate branch of the river (the B-family scenarios of 1972). The no-growth-no-problem scenario (B1) was clearly implausible as economies, fully recovered from the 1971 recession, boomed. The three-miracles scenario (B3) remained just that—three supply miracles. Finally, our discussions with governments about the impending crisis had allowed us to conclude that their reaction would occur only after the fact. (Obviously, we hadn't yet learned how to affect governmental microcosms.)

Because the B-branch of the river was dammed, we needed to explore other potential streams that dovetailed with management's current optimism, an optimism based on the booming economy of late 1972 and early 1973—in which growth exceeded that of any period since the Korean War. In an oil company having an affair with expansion, many executives were naturally reluctant to slow or suspend the expansion of refineries, the building of tankers, and so forth. In response, we created two "phantom" scenarios—alternatives to our main scenarios but ones we considered illusions. In Phantom Scenario I, we assumed a delay of 5 years in the onset of the disruption; in Phantom II, 15 years. (These represented typical times needed to first, bring a new oil facility into service and second, amortize it.) These phantom scenarios were used to measure the "regret" Shell would feel if it planned for a discontinuity that never occurred for 5 or even 15 more years.

Only two developments could delay the inevitable and both were ruled out: (1) the discovery of new Middle East-sized oil reserves in an area that would have no problem in absorbing revenues, or (2) political or military seizure and control of producers by consuming countries.

Exhibit IX   **A new worldview**

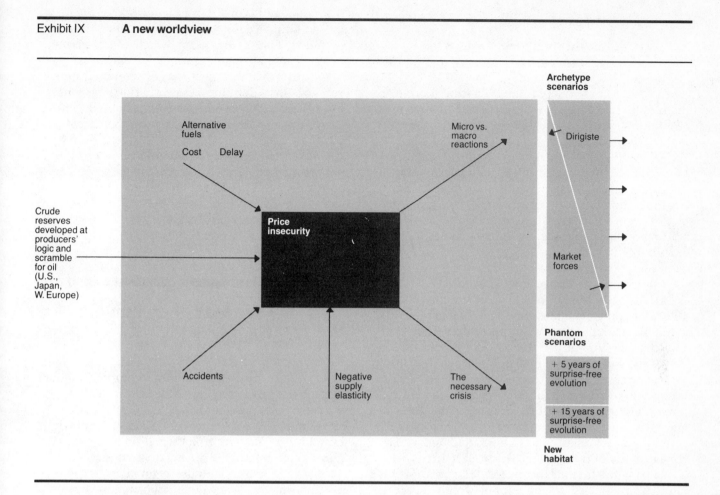

More than water on a stone

On the surface, the 1973 scenarios seemed much like the A-scenarios constructed in 1972. Driven by a new sense of urgency, however, we saw them in a different light. The time we had to anticipate, prepare for, and respond to the new environment had shrunk greatly.

More important, we wanted the 1973 scenarios to be more than water on a stone: we wanted to change our managers' view of reality. The first step was to question and destroy their existing view of the world in which oil demand expanded in orderly and predictable fashion, and Shell routinely could add oil fields, refineries, tankers, and marketing outlets. In fact, we had been at this job of destruction now for several years.

But exposing and invalidating an obsolete worldview is not where scenario analysis stops. Reconstructing a new model is the most important job and is the responsibility of the managers themselves. The planners' job is to engage the decision makers' interest and participation in this reconstruction. We listen carefully to their needs and give them the highest quality materials to use in making decisions. The planners will succeed, however, only if they can securely link the new realities of the outside world—the unfolding business environment—to the managers' microcosm. Good scenarios supply this vital "bridge"; they must encompass both managers' concerns and external reality. Otherwise, no one will bother to cross the bridge.

If the planners design the package well, managers will use scenarios to construct a new model of reality by selecting from them those elements they believe relevant to their business world. Because they have been making decisions—and have a long track record to show that they're good at it—they may, of course, not see any relevant elements. Or they may go with what their "gut" tells them. But that should not discourage the planner who is drawing up the scenario.

Just as managers had to change their worldview, so planners had to change the way they viewed the planning process. So often, planning is divorced from the managers for whom it is intended. We came to understand that making the scenarios relevant required a keener knowledge of decision makers and their microcosm than we had ever imagined. In later years, we built some bridges that did not get used. The reason for this failure was always that we did not design scenarios that responded to managers' deepest concerns.

Building blocks for new microcosms

In developing the 1973 scenarios, we realized that if managers were to reframe their view of reality, they would need a clear overview of a new model. *Exhibit IX*, one way to portray that model, summarizes the anticipated business environment and its key elements: the predetermined events, which are shown on the left, and the major discontinuities, which are shown in the center.

We focused attention on the following features of the business environment (shown in *Exhibit IX*):

☐   Alternative fuels, which we could develop only very slowly. Even under a wartime crash development program, none could be available before the 1980s. We analyzed the cost in three stages. First, even though other fuels might replace oil for generating power and steam in large industrial settings, the oil-producing nations would not be impressed. On the contrary, they welcomed the alternative of coal and nuclear power in what they considered low-value markets. Second, oil used for heating was a different story. Burning coal was not a satisfactory alternative. You would have to gasify or transform coal into electricity, with accompanying thermodynamic loss. The price for this alternative was high; the price for oil would not exceed this threshold in the near future. The third possibility, oil used in transport, had an even higher fuel cost than oil used for heating and was obviously irrelevant.

☐   Accidents, which included both political and internal and physical incidents, are events that any oil executive considers a matter of course. In the same way, a Filipino knows that a roof must be built carefully; even though the weather in the Philippines is usually balmy, typhoons are frequent enough that the only uncertainty is when the roof's strength will be tested.

☐   Negative supply elasticity, which means that unlike other commodities the supply of oil does not increase with increases in its price, at least for a number of years. On the contrary, the higher the price, the lower the volume of oil it would be in the interest of the major exporting countries to produce.

As planners at the center of a diverse group of companies, we faced a special problem beyond the construction of a new worldview. We had to make its message useful not only to managing directors but also to operating companies from Canada to Germany, Japan to Australia. And yet the dramatic changes we anticipated would affect each differently. What basic message could we convey to all of them?

To construct a framework for the message, we borrowed the concept of archetypes from psychology. Just as we often view individuals as composites of archetypes (for example, part introvert and part extrovert), so we developed governmental archetypes to help us examine differing national responses. In our view, nations would favor either a market-force or government-intervention (*dirigiste*) approach. No country would follow one path exclusively. We expected, for example, that West Germany's response would be more market oriented, whereas France's would be more *dirigiste*. We analyzed the actions anticipated under each archetypal response in terms of price increases, taxes, alternative fuel development, and regulations by market class.

We led the managers to water...

While we didn't fully comprehend that influencing managers required a tailor-made fit between the scenarios and their deepest concerns, we knew intuitively that events in 1973 gave us this fit in several ways. The arrows on the right side of *Exhibit IX* symbolize four of the implications stressed.

We told our upstream managers, engaged in exploration and production, that the unthinkable was going to happen: "Be careful! You are about to lose the major part of your concessions and mining rents." The traditional profit base in the upstream world would be lost and new relationships would have to be developed between the company and producing nations.

To the downstream world of refiners, transporters, and marketers, we said something equally alarming: "Prepare! You are about to become a low-growth industry." Oil demand had always grown more rapidly than GNP, something Shell's management took for granted. In the past, we did not have to consider the consequences of overinvestment; one or two years of normal market growth would cure any premature moves. Now oil consumption in industrial countries would increase at rates less than the increase in GNP, and Shell would have to develop new instincts and reflexes to function in a low-growth world.

A third serious implication was the need to further decentralize the decision-making and strategic process. One basic strategy would no longer be valid for operating companies in most parts of the world. Shell companies had generally – and successfully – aimed for a higher share of conversion in refineries than did the competition. Now we understood that the energy shock would affect each nation so differently that each would have to respond independently. Shell, which was already decentralized compared with other oil majors, did in fact decentralize further, enabling it to adjust faster to the turbulence experienced later. (For some time now, it has been the most decentralized of all the major oil companies.)

Finally, we made managers see that because we didn't know when the disruption would come, they should prepare for it in different phases of the business cycle. We developed three simulations. In the first, the oil shock occurred before the cyclical downturn; in the second, the events were simultaneous; and in the third, the oil shock followed the downturn. These simulations led us to prepare for a far more serious economic decline than might otherwise have been expected.

...and most finally drank

We hit planning pay dirt with the 1973 scenarios because they met the deepest concerns of managers. If any managers were not fully convinced, the events of October soon made them believers. We had set out to produce not a scenario booklet simply summarizing views but a change in the way managers view their world. Only when the oil embargo began could we appreciate the power of scenarios—power that becomes apparent when the world overturns, power that has immense and immediate value in a large, decentralized organization.

Strategies are the product of a worldview. When the world changes, managers need to share some common view of the new world. Otherwise, decentralized strategic decisions will result in management anarchy. Scenarios express and communicate this common view, a shared understanding of the new realities to all parts of the organization.

Decentralized management in worldwide operating companies can adapt and use that view for strategic decisions appropriate to its varied circumstances. Its initiative is not limited by instructions dictated from the center but facilitated and freed by a broad framework; all will speak the same language in adapting their operations to a new business environment. Companies from Finland to New Zealand now knew what "the rapids" meant, were alert to the implications of producer logic, and recognized the need to prepare for a new environment.

From studying evolution, we learn how an animal suited to one environment must become a new animal to survive when the environment undergoes severe change. We believed that Shell would have to become a new animal to function in a new world. Business-as-usual decisions would no longer suffice.

In the next installment, I will discuss how we adapted the technique to develop scenarios for the short term. As the time span between decisions steadily became shorter, this refinement became necessary. ▽

Reprint 85516

Ten specific management techniques that can improve any company's performance

What Working for a Japanese Company Taught Me

by John E. Rehfeld

Back in the late 1970s, as a consultant to several Japanese computer giants, I read everything I could about Japanese business. It was all very interesting—interesting, but not particularly useful. When I became a line manager in 1981, I realized how little of what I'd read had any practical value. I couldn't control interest rates, the education system, or the culture. Wasn't there something to learn from the Japanese that I could actually apply in my own managerial role?

> **I learned right away *what* they do. It took a while to appreciate *why*.**

Having spent the past ten years working for Japanese companies, I can now answer that question. As an insider, I've discovered more than ten specific management techniques the Japanese use to run their businesses. I've also come to understand why these techniques are so effective; I've seen them change people's behavior—including my own. And I've learned that many, though not all, of these approaches are equally effective in the United States.

My "research lab" has been Toshiba America, where I was vice president and general manager of its computer division for nine years, and Seiko Instruments USA, where I have been president of U.S. operations since 1989. Toshiba America and Seiko Instruments USA are U.S. companies, have mostly American employees, and compete in the U.S. market, but they have strong cultural and financial ties to Japan.

I have had close relationships with the Japanese managers assigned to me and with those to whom I reported in Japan. I have seen how they manage their own people, American employees, customers and vendors, and the external marketplace. I've heard the president of Toshiba America say, as we discussed some problems with product quality, "This is not Japanese quality." And I've heard Japanese managers say, when talking about problems with an American employee, "We must help this person overcome his weaknesses."

John E. Rehfeld is president and chief operating officer of Seiko Instruments USA, Inc., of Torrance, California. From 1981 to 1989, he was vice president and general manager of Toshiba America's computer business. Before that, he was a market-research consultant to Japanese high-technology companies.

From this vantage point, I've seen how powerful seemingly simple things like six-month budget cycles, consensus decision making, and *kaizen*, or continuous improvement, can be, especially in combination. While non-Japanese managers are familiar with—and may even practice—some of the typically Japanese management techniques, rarely do they practice them all.

I want to encourage non-Japanese managers to put aside economic, cultural, and trade issues for the moment and learn from what I've seen the Japanese do every day.

Welcome to Japanese Management

When I was hired in 1981 to help Toshiba capture the U.S. computer market, I was full of ambition and energy. I needed it, since all I had to work with were four Japanese engineers, one American secretary, and two misfit personal computers the U.S. market didn't want. The two CPM-based, 8-bit CPU personal computers could not run any U.S. software and were hardly elegant machines. (CPM is the operating system for the 8-bit computer.) The trade press, in fact, described the PCs as "rugged tanks."

Within a month, IBM made the whole CPM world obsolete with the introduction of the IBM PC DOS machine using 16-bit CPU (central processing unit) technology. We had a difficult product to sell, and problems of culture and credibility made it hard to convince Toshiba's Japanese engineers to respond. The problems seemed insurmountable. Frankly, I

I saw how the Japanese went from an obsolete product to a thriving business.

thought Toshiba would fail and abandon the U.S. market. But it didn't. We overcame the initial business setbacks and over the next three years introduced a better quality dot-matrix printer and went on to build a $75 million printer business against such formidable opponents as Epson, NEC, and Oki. We then reentered the PC market with a laptop computer and gained a leading share in that market. By the time I left Toshiba in 1989, 350 American and two Japanese employees were supporting annual sales of $400 million.

Perseverance and patient capital helped, but I also attribute Toshiba's success to the management approaches that allowed the company to learn and stay on track. Let me explain how I came to accept—and even appreciate—these approaches and why I think non-Japanese managers should use them too.

Budget for Six Months

When I went to work for Toshiba, I immediately had to adjust to a 6-month budgeting cycle. The Japanese fiscal year generally runs from April through March. Although a full-year budget is prepared in January or February, only the first 6 months are approved—the A period. The B part is modified based on the initial results in the A period and is formally approved in August or September.

Like any U.S. businessperson, I had come in with a 12-month mind-set, so the budgeting periods seemed to come up too fast. I had no sooner developed a budget and countermeasures to correct variances than I was going through it all again. I was giving twice as many performance reviews and awarding bonuses twice as often.

To me, 6-month budgeting was just twice as much work. But after three or four fiscal periods, I began to appreciate it. I came to welcome the opportunity to change the budget because the world had changed so much in 6 months (remember, this was the PC business!). And having two deadlines each year leaves less room for procrastination. If you're slipping from the budget after the first quarter and you know you have only 3 months instead of 9 to get back on plan, you work harder to figure out what to do. There's a greater sense of urgency to hit the target.

Of course, budgets are also a planning tool. If the budget becomes meaningless during the course of the year, the company is like a ship without a rudder. And if you're running a company with several divisions, the effect is cumulative. If, say, three divisions are each off by 20%, it's pretty hard for senior executives to know what to expect. If, on the other hand, the divisions are pretty much on track, management has some control.

Also, each new budget gave us a chance to wipe the slate clean and start over, which was good for motivation because it allowed managers to adjust goals that no longer seemed achievable. All managers miss their budgets. But if you slip so much that you lose hope of reaching your target, you lose motivation. You know you don't stand a chance of making it, so you give up.

When I arrived at Seiko Instruments, its seven divisions were using a 12-month budget cycle. One of the computer peripherals divisions at Seiko Instruments, which was in a particularly volatile industry, was so far off the plan that managers weren't even referring to the original budget. They had given up on it and were putting up a new set of numbers every month rather than concentrating on developing and implementing countermeasures to minimize the negative variances to budget.

Since then, all of our divisions have switched to a 6-month budget. This year, the same division was off budget again – but it was off for 3 months instead of 10. Knowing that the end of the fiscal period was just 3 months away, the managers immediately developed countermeasures to minimize the variances to budget. Midyear, they reset the budget and came up with additional countermeasures. If they had still been using a 12-month budget, they would have been directionless again. But by stopping to ask why they were off and then making adjustments, they put a rudder on their ship. The division used to be 30% off budget, but now it's maybe 10% off – which is something you can get your arms around and fix.

When I tell my U.S. peers about 6-month budgeting, I get one of two reactions. Either they say we spend too much time planning, or they ask why we don't use a quarterly plan. A quarter is too short a time to turn the ship. Besides, it would be too time consuming to create the plan, get it approved, communicate it to everyone, and start performing against it every 3 months. Six months is a good compromise. You ensure that the budget is realistic, but you don't spend all your time on the budget process. Having lived with it for nearly a decade, I think it feels just about right.

Fix the Problem, Not the Blame

When I say many people miss their business plans, I include myself. From the first month on at Toshiba, I missed the plan. We had a personal computer the market didn't want; we couldn't make any changes without getting engineering in Japan to approve and implement them; and management in Japan didn't fully understand the U.S. market. The budget called for $3 million in sales in the first six months. We

shipped approximately $3 million worth of equipment – but we got paid for only about half. Since we were unable to make the engineering upgrades we had promised, the rest came back. The next year the plan called for $10 million. We almost made those numbers, but the product mix – and profit – was not as planned. We made it with printers; the PC sales never really got off the ground.

I was doing the best I could under the circumstances, but I expected big trouble when I met with the Japanese higher-ups. They represented manufacturing, product development, and the money, and I represented sales and marketing. Everyone was under stress. I was prepared for a knock-down-drag-out fight over who was to blame for our lousy performance.

Those early meetings were another source of insight into Japanese management. When we got together to talk about why we were underperforming, no one got emotional. The discussions were always calm, and the focus was always on solving the problems. No one seemed the least bit interested in laying blame. Rather than chastising me and putting me on the defensive, they talked to me about what was going wrong and how to fix it.

I immediately felt that I was part of the team and worked that much harder to get us out of our predicament. I realized that others in the company had a lot of trust in me, and I wanted to live up to it.

I can't help but think about what would have happened in a typical U.S. company. When things go wrong, the instinct is to find a scapegoat. I probably would have been fired and replaced. And the problems would still be there for the new person to deal with.

Don't Rest on Your Laurels

My managers and I really knocked ourselves out during those early years at Toshiba, with little to show for it. Even though I didn't get beat up about it, I was under a lot of pressure to make the goals. We started to achieve the budget in the third year, and we continued to make it for something like nine periods in a row.

I felt great that all the stress and hard work was finally paying off, and I kept waiting for my efforts to be acknowledged. But I never got a thank-you. I got some satisfaction from the business performance itself, but I was frustrated and discouraged that no one back at headquarters seemed to recognize how far we'd come. My staff was discouraged too and complained to me, "We do this great job, but we never get a thank-you. Do the Japanese think we're their slaves?"

I finally gave up hope of getting praise. I figured it was just a cultural thing. But little by little, I began to understand what was behind it. The Japanese simply are not interested only in the absolute results; they are equally interested in the process and in how you can do it better next time. I didn't have a name for this seemingly negative environment back then, but now I see it as part of the process of kaizen, or continuous improvement.

Kaizen is typically referred to in the context of quality control, but the Japanese apply it broadly. In many areas, they not only *plan* something and *do* it but also stop to *see* the result to determine how it could be done better. American managers, on the other hand, tend to be task-oriented. They create a goal and set out to attain it. Americans interpret the *see* part as a report card—a pat on the back or an admission of mistakes. For the Japanese, it is an opportunity to reflect and learn.

I have a friend who is responsible for two factories, one in Japan and one in the United States. He explained why the factory in Japan always outperforms the one in the United States: "They both set the same target, and they both may hit it. But when the Japanese hit it, they keep going, whereas the Americans tend to stop and rest on their laurels

> Now I know why I never got a thank-you: the Japanese value the process, not the result.

before pursuing the next goal. So in the end, the Japanese achieve more." They continuously strive for perfection with the goal of achieving excellence.

I'm not saying that it's a good idea to withhold praise. The Japanese style is very frustrating for many non-Japanese, especially those who have little direct contact with the business plan and therefore don't derive direct satisfaction from achieving the numbers. Even for me, there were times when positive feedback would have boosted my enthusiasm and morale at Toshiba. Most people respond better to constructive criticism when it is balanced with some thanks and compliments. But the constant striving to do better and to learn from your successes and failures is an important step toward superior performance.

The compulsion to look for ways to improve paid off at Toshiba. One common promotional tool in the PC business is dealer demonstration programs, whereby you offer dealers a free unit for buying a certain number of products. The dealers have to keep the demos in the store for a specified period of time before they sell them. Like most Americans, I started out designing the program, getting the units out, and then going on to the next thing. My Japanese colleagues would always remind me to *see* if the program was working. Improving a million-dollar program, even a little, saves a lot of money.

Stay Focused

Just as the fascination with deal making permeates U.S. business, the sense of sticking to the knitting characterizes Japanese business. Americans love to make deals. The highly publicized large salaries and jackpot payoffs of the 1980s further encouraged this get-rich-quick deal making. Japanese businesspeople prefer to improve incrementally something they're already doing—just like Japanese artists. The vast majority of Japanese artists pick a subject or a style and stick with it forever. Yoshiharu Kimura, a woodblock artist, has done nothing but birds for 25 years; another, printmaker Shigeki Kuroda, has for 10 years been depicting only bicycles and umbrellas in every conceivable permutation. By staying focused and by applying the technique of kaizen, these artists consistently improve their work.

It was the same thing at Toshiba. We questioned how we could improve, but always in the context of what we were already doing. We were never drawn off track, even when attractive opportunities arose. In 1987, I was approached by an entrepreneur with an intriguing plan for a laptop computer with an Apple Macintosh base. He had a solid scheme for solving the legal and technical issues. When I proposed this plan to top management, I received a polite but emphatic no. Toshiba R&D management people in Japan said that their mission was to be king of the PC laptop, meaning the IBM-compatible laptop. And that was that. They didn't want to dilute Toshiba's efforts by going into another area. Maybe there were other reasons not to go into the Macintosh area, but we never discussed them. It was understood that the Macintosh distribution channels, software philosophy, and user base were simply too far away from our main business.

The Japanese not only passed up seemingly attractive options but also pursued seemingly unattractive ones simply because of how they defined the boundaries of the business. For instance, Toshiba got into the floppy disk drive business in 1987 when everyone else was getting out. Toshiba was in the computer business, and floppies were a way to add value to that business. The company entered that market by brute force. Maybe Toshiba is making money on floppies now, but at the time, no venture capitalist "deal maker" would have backed that decision.

I've also seen the stick-to-the-knitting mind-set played out at Seiko Instruments. For the past 50 years, the company has been one of the world's largest manufacturers of quality watches. A dozen years ago, the company decided to diversify beyond its relatively mature category. But instead of buying other companies or inventing totally new products, either of which it could have done, the company looked inward to its own products – those proprietary technologies and applications it knew best. It commercialized those and now has more than 15 product lines ranging from precision assembly robots to electronic components to scientific test instruments.

So sticking to the knitting is a way of channeling energy, of putting blinders on, and of defining the realm in which you're going to play. To Americans, it probably seems boring. They see all these other exciting things going on in the world and know the company has the resources to pursue them. It takes a lot of discipline to ignore them and stay focused. But after a while the discipline becomes automatic. People who have been in a company, a division, or a department for their whole careers understand that they're there to make the best computers and to sell them on a worldwide basis. It's just instilled in them.

You could argue that it's wrong to be narrow-minded, but I think the more focused approach is better in the long run. It takes the emphasis off making deals and puts it on figuring out how to sell more, bring costs down, gain market share, and add more value for the customer. So Toshiba looks for ways to expand the basic technology its products are based on, like the color liquid-crystal display monitor. It tries to expand geographically or improve the product cycle by offering postsales support, always building on the core business.

Quantify Everything

Another frustration for an American is the Japanese insistence on quantifying everything, even intangible things. It seemed like an obsession to me at first. During my second year at Toshiba, we started to experience success with the dot-matrix printer business, and we started launching some marketing programs to build our active dealer base by providing them with demo printers. About 18 months into the program, we were seeing some success, and we started to have some money for promotions. We had maybe $300,000 that we wanted to use to get demonstration units out to the dealers. I discussed the program with the Japanese assistant general manager, Shigechika Takeuchi, now president of Apple Computer, Japan. As an aside, I reported to Tokyo,

and he reported to me, but he communicated regularly with Tokyo. He was sort of my nag and "shadow." (For more on shadow managers, see the insert on "Japanese Blindspot: Outsiders.")

I can still picture Mr. Takeuchi sitting in my office where we were planning our first demo program. I vividly remember it because it was so exciting – the first tangible indication of our success. We really had a product that the channel and the end users wanted, and we were able to do something constructive to broaden our distribution. This excitement was dampened, however, by Takeuchi's obsession with the numbers. He kept asking, "How much are you going to spend? What are you going to accomplish? How much more are you going to sell next month, next quarter, next year as a result?" I was convinced that these things couldn't be measured. I said, "You can't tell how much you're going to sell next year because of this program. That's ridiculous." After all, this was marketing. But the more I resisted, the more he insisted that we do it. And soon we were putting numbers on the white board.

I still believe that the numbers you attach to marketing programs are not an end in themselves; you can't predict exactly the sales a demo program will generate. And public relations and corporate citizenship programs are even harder to justify in numerical terms. In short, I think the Japanese take "management by the numbers" to the extreme. I guess it's because they don't completely trust personal judgment – especially when they're depending on *gaijin* (outsiders) – and want to avoid personal risk taking. And maybe, too, it's because numbers are a universal language.

When I missed the target, my manager wanted to help me – not blame me.

Japanese Blindspot: Outsiders

The Japanese draw sharp distinctions between insiders and outsiders. The concept of insider starts with the family and extends to the school, the company, and the country. The result is a strong "old boy" network in each company that makes it hard for outsiders to be accepted.

The old boy network gains strength as groups of managers progress through the company together. Every group entering Toshiba is given a class-year designation, and people take it to heart. I've heard senior managers at Toshiba referring to other managers within the company as their classmates, even though they entered the class 30 years ago.

Many Japanese companies will not hire outsiders (people from other companies) for any position higher than an entry-level one, even when it works to the company's disadvantage. Toshiba went into the laser-printer business after several other manufacturers had already developed and introduced products. But rather than hire top engineers from those other companies, it reinvented the wheel. The product development process moved along so slowly because of the lack of expertise that the company missed an important opportunity.

The Japanese are also notorious for limiting the advancement of non-Japanese managers. No matter how long a non-Japanese works for a Japanese company, he or she is still considered an outsider. It's a black-and-white issue with nothing in between. This, of course, deprives the company of the experience and knowledge that an outsider can contribute.

Some people point to the use of "shadow managers" as a clear indication of the lower status of non-Japanese managers. Shadow managers play the role of informally communicating with Tokyo, often performing *nemawashi*, which literally translates to cutting the roots before you plant the tree. What it really means is informing Tokyo of what is going on and what requests will be made. It is much like a lobbying effort that precedes a formal plan or proposal. I've always experienced this role as a positive one. But I've heard that other Japanese companies use shadow managers to relay what amounts to orders from Tokyo through the assistant general manager to the general manager and then to the division, effectively depriving the non-Japanese executive of any real decision-making power.

While I still believe that subjective judgment has its place, I've come to appreciate the value of trying to quantify things you know are uncertain. The numbers force you to make estimates and to compare relative alternatives, and they give you something to measure the outcome against. They impose a certain rigor that can help you consider different options. If you're seeding 700 PC units at about $2,100 each, which is the size and cost of a typical demo program, you want to have some idea of how long those units are going to be used as demos there (dealers have a way of selling them). How many more units will dealers sell because they have the demo there? How many sales will they miss by not having them? It's amazing how many problems become clearer when you try to break them down into numbers.

Now I'm the guy at the white board telling others to put it in numbers. It usually takes a lot of arm-twisting, which I'm willing to do. I recall having to push one American field service manager at Seiko Instruments, who was proposing to invest $100,000 and increase staff by 15%, to improve field service. He kept giving qualitative measures of what he wanted to accomplish. I constantly had to ask him to give me quantitative targets. This forced him to refine and justify his thinking and programs. It was a painful process. Although it seems to be second nature for the Japanese, it is something most Americans don't do naturally.

Know the Whole Person

Having spent many an evening at *Ginza* restaurants and hostess clubs, like every business visitor to Japan, I was struck by how easily the Japanese can change gears. During the day, they grappled intensely with heavy-duty business problems, but at night they drop the subject completely and socialize. Six o'clock begins a second day, one in which conversations about business are taboo. Once when I started talking about business during a golf lunch, my colleagues reminded me that it was "personal" time.

Reserving strictly social time forces businesspeople to get to know each other on a different and much more personal level. They get to know each other as whole people. I've seen how important that is to business relationships. It builds trust and makes communication much easier.

I can think of a couple of situations that illustrate the point. When my first manager, Mr. Hirai, learned that the senior manager he worked with in Tokyo was leaving for an assignment in Germany, he was very disappointed. "Mr. Sato and I have worked together for so long that we know how each other thinks," he explained. "I can anticipate what he's thinking and feeling."

I had the same kind of relationship with Dan Crane, my vice president of computer marketing at Toshiba. He and I shared a lot of experiences in Japan—from drinking beer in Roppongi to climbing Mount Fuji. So we trusted each other and never had to waste energy wondering what the other really meant or worrying about hidden agendas.

Japanese Blindspot: Women

Japanese companies are unwilling to invest in training their female employees. As a result, this highly educated part of the work force is terribly underused. I've often seen very competent women who have graduated from the top universities do little more than serve tea. In the 15 years that I've been closely involved with Japanese companies, most of the "career moves" I've seen women make are to graduate slowly from tea servers to note takers to administrative assistants.

Management does not consider training and development of female workers a sound investment because it expects the women to leave the workplace at an early age to marry and raise a family, as they have traditionally done. If a woman leaves the work force when she is about 25 years old, it is difficult for her to return. The Japanese culture and infrastructure do not support women who wish to return to work after having children. There are no day-care centers or babysitting services, and such women are looked down on. Of course, there are some highly publicized exceptions where women have taken strong leadership roles in Japan. But attitudes and institutions overwhelmingly work against the effective use of women professionals.

That trust was especially important during the tense time when Toshiba was ready to get back into the U.S. computer business after having de-emphasized it several years earlier. It seemed obvious to me that our division should market the computer; but

> ## We didn't talk business on the golf course. That was personal time.

the Japanese always explore the alternatives, so a task force was formed to analyze it. Dan was on the task force with many Japanese managers from Tokyo, and I wasn't. I could have found that situation very threatening, but I had confidence in Dan's judgment. I knew that the decision the task force reached would be rational. As it turns out, the decision was in favor of our division—which proves my point!

I can't say I'm prepared to go out every night with my American colleagues—and I doubt that they would want to. But when we do get together outside of regular business hours, I try not to work on business problems. We talk about families and sports and other things that help us get to know each other better. It helps us get along during the business day.

Get People to Buy into the Decision

This issue of getting back into computers after our initial failure demonstrates the Japanese approach to decision making: try to get everyone to agree. This is the Japanese consensus decision making we all hear about. Toshiba wasn't the only company in deep trouble because its computers couldn't run Lotus and weren't IBM compatible. Every Japanese company had made the same mistake, as had Texas Instruments, Digital Equipment Corporation, Wang Laboratories, and Hewlett-Packard.

At a certain point, it was obvious to us at Toshiba America that we had to be IBM compatible. We had been living and breathing the U.S. market. But we had two other groups to contend with—the Japanese engineers in the Tokyo factory R&D and the Tokyo marketing group. They weren't sure. So we formed a study team, led by McKinsey, to go through the painstaking process of talking to distributors, dealers, and end users, gathering data, and deciding what we needed. Guess what the task force concluded: we needed to be IBM compatible.

The purpose of the task force, of course, was to get the others to buy in, which seemed to me a royal waste of time. But I learned that in the end, it wasn't. When the other groups bought in, they bought in

My VP and I trusted each other completely because we had literally climbed mountains together.

with a vengeance, and their commitment more than made up for the slow decision making. When we finally settled on the idea of "being blue" (IBM's color), all the players felt they owned the idea. We were all equally determined to be "brighter blue."

That's how we arrived at the idea of a full-featured, IBM-compatible laptop computer. We were the first major company to come out with a successful laptop. We lost more time in the beginning getting everybody focused, but things moved quickly after that.

With my American managers, I'm somewhat less concerned about reaching 100% consensus agreement. I've learned through experience that collaborative decision making works virtually as well as the consensus approach. While consensus requires 100% effort to achieve 100% "buy in," collaboration requires only 20% effort to achieve 80% buy in. I talk or collaborate with everyone because I've seen the importance of owning a decision; I know people want to be heard and not dictated to. But I have limits about how much time I can afford to take. In the United States, the majority rules, so no one seems to expect 100% agreement anyway.

Empower the International Sales Group

Sorting out the Japanese organizational structure is a challenge – job titles are not equivalent to those in the United States. There are many dotted lines and gray areas of responsibility. Most of my early dealings were with the president of Toshiba America. But soon after, I had a lot of communication with a group of engineers from Japan who seemed to have similar business interests. I wondered who those guys were.

"Those guys" were part of the international sales and marketing group. The ISM is highly influential and important. In fact, the president of the U.S. subsidiary reports to the general manager of the ISM. And the general manager of the ISM reports almost directly to the president of the whole company, with maybe one person in between.

The ISM is responsible for global business development outside Japan. In essence, it buys product from the Japanese and resells it to the U.S. and other international subsidiaries at a markup, which covers its salaries and creates a pool for investing in geographic growth elsewhere. When we started, the ISM had money to invest in us. Then after we got going, the ISM took money from us and invested it in Europe and Canada.

But the significance of the ISM is that it focuses solely on developing business internationally and has the organizational clout to make things happen. It goes out and researches other markets, identifies existing products or product development opportunities, and then goes back to Japan and spearheads the development effort. That's exactly what happened with the laptop. The ISM was on the task force that decided we wanted to be brighter blue. Then Mr. Hataya, who headed the group, led the laptop product development in Japan. It is interesting to note that although NEC is the compatibility standard in the Japanese market, Toshiba did not develop an NEC-compatible laptop. That goes to show how much power the ISM has.

Because of the ISM, I basically had two bosses. I reported directly to the president of Toshiba America, who approved the business plan and evaluated the

First international sales gave us money – then they took it away.

fiscal period business performance. But I also had a dotted line – a very thick, black dotted line – to Mr. Hataya. He was interested in long-term business development in addition to meeting the current fiscal business plan. So each of my bosses had a different perspective. One manager was looking at the day-to-day P&L, and the other was taking a back-road view of product development, spin-offs, and global market development.

This arrangement gave me the flexibility to subordinate short-term pressures to long-term market development. If I wanted to invest current profits to expand the market instead of making a higher percentage profit, for instance, I could always make my case informally to Mr. Hataya, who could then informally influence the president.

Although many U.S. companies have international sales and marketing organizations, those organizations don't have the same power, probably because company leaders have only recently recognized the importance of actively pursuing international markets where stiff competition against the best in all areas of the world ensures that they remain world-class. Typically, world-class companies should have more than a third of sales outside their home market.

I attribute the ISM's success to two things: first, the product manager is highly empowered; second, the product manager is a senior manager with more than 25 years of experience in the company, a wide range of experiences, and a broad network of colleagues he knows and trusts.

Visit Customers, Build Market Share

When I presented my budget, I was always pressed hard to justify head count, for two reasons: first, head count sooner or later leads to higher fixed expenses; and second, the Japanese don't believe in layoffs, so they would rather be conservative. On the other hand, advertising and travel expenses were easy to justify – advertising because theoretically it yields market share, and travel because it encourages visits to customers. I know that in U.S. companies, you're always trying to schedule several things when you're making a long trip. Consequently, the trip inevitably gets postponed. But for the Japanese, having only one meeting is no reason not to go.

I was amazed at how easily the Japanese would jump on an airplane to visit a customer. I could always get the president of Toshiba America to fly to Texas, even for a one-hour meeting. I do my share of flying too. Recently, I flew from California to Greenville, South Carolina for one two-hour meeting.

At Seiko Instruments, we have guidelines for how much time we should spend visiting customers, either at their offices or at trade shows, and we tie customer contact to the management bonus plan, even for top managers. General management should spend 20% of its time with customers, for instance, sales management 40%, operations management 30%, field service management 20%, marketing 25%, and engineering 5%. This is one way to reinforce the idea that customers matter.

Market share also matters. The conventional wisdom is that market share is good because you sell more, and therefore you can make big capital investments in the manufacturing process. That's true, of course. But there's also a less obvious advantage.

Market share gives you visibility, so more people will hear about the product through word of mouth. Many people buy a technical product because they have confidence in it – it was recommended by a friend, or they saw someone else using it. And exist-

> ## Travel expenses are easy to justify. Customers are worth it.

ing customers are already sold on your brand, your quality, and your service, so it's relatively easy to sell them an add-on or upgrade.

Some U.S. companies have de-emphasized market share, and they've lost visibility. After a while, they're no longer a force in the market. One New England photographic company comes quickly to mind, but there are lots of other examples.

The Japanese don't like businesses that aren't profitable, so when they talk about investing in market share, they're not talking about negative P&L. They want the business to make a "healthy" profit, which means enough money so you can still break even if you have a setback. But it's okay to make a few percentage points less and spend money on promotions and other things that will build market share – things that look like an expense but translate into an investment.

I had a good technique for making this case. I would prepare a 6-month budget with "normal" operational P&L. In addition, I would show projected sales for the 18 months beyond that budget. Then I would prepare a second "investment" budget with lower P&L results. Along with it, I showed the 18-month follow-on sales, which were enough to justify the lower P&L that I was attempting to sell.

Granted, U.S. companies have to produce quarterly profits to bolster the stock price, but I think it's a matter of pitching it to investors the right way.

Demand Active, Informed Directors

Japanese companies have an important operational resource U.S. companies generally do not: the board of directors, which consists of 15 to 20 of the company's top operating managers and a few outsiders who are closely associated with the company. Managers become eligible for the board in their early fifties and have a few opportunities to be elected. The grapevine is always abuzz with conjecture about who will or will not make it.

Those who do make it sit on the board for a few years and then retire. The constant turnover of members ensures that the board doesn't get stale. The fact that the members are drawn from the ranks of people who have many years of experience ensures that they are committed and knowledgeable.

So when Japanese boards get deeply involved in strategic and operating decisions – as we all do – they have a lot to contribute. Board members are really an extension of top divisional line management, and the constituency of the board is really the employees. Therefore, the point of view is on operations and building value in the core business rather than financial or legal maneuvering and deal making.

I can appreciate that outside directors bring an important perspective to U.S. boards, but outsiders have neither enough time nor financial incentive to understand the company deeply. And because the CEO usually appoints them, they tend to be reluctant to stand up to management. It's the company's loss.

Let me repeat the disclaimer that the approaches I've described here are not unique to Japan. In fact, my observations are consistent with the new wave of management thinking in the United States. And let me reiterate that I don't think non-Japanese managers should do everything that Japanese managers do. For instance, I don't recommend 100% consensus decision making, especially in crisis situations, nor do I think managers should neglect to thank people for a job well done.

My message is simple: the way to make great leaps is to take many small steps, consistently, every day.

Reprint 90607

"And keep in mind, the entire time, we want to avoid any appearance of impropriety."

CARTOON BY LEO CULLUM

Pitfalls in evaluating risky projects

Good analysis depends not only on techniques, but also on key assumptions

James E. Hodder and Henry E. Riggs

Recent critics of American business are wont to claim that our managers rely too heavily on a few financial techniques in weighing major investment decisions. Calculation of discounted cash flows, internal rates of return, and net present values, say the critics, is inherently biased against long-term investments. According to the authors of this article, the technicians, not the techniques, are the problem. Discounting procedures are not inherently biased if management sets realistic hurdle rates and examines carefully its own assumptions. Unfortunately, many DCF analyses of risky projects are overly simplistic and ignore three critical issues that managers and decision makers should consider: the effects of inflation, the different levels of uncertainty in different phases of a project, and management's own ability to mitigate risk.

Mr. Hodder is assistant professor of industrial engineering and engineering management at Stanford University. His teaching and research have focused on capital budgeting and international hedging decisions.

Mr. Riggs is professor of industrial engineering and engineering management and vice president for development at Stanford University. Before joining the university in 1974, he worked for 15 years in industry in various financial positions. Riggs is the author of many publications on accounting and finance and of the recent book, Managing High-Technology Companies *(Belmont, California, Lifetime Learnings Publications, a division of Wadsworth, Inc., 1983).*

In recent years, the leaders of American companies have been barraged with attacks on their investment policies. Critics accuse American executives of shortsightedness and point out that managers in Japan and Europe often fix their vision on more distant horizons. Here, it is claimed, managers pay too much attention to quarterly earnings reports and not enough to such basic elements of industrial strength as research and development. Some analysts see the root of this problem in the tendency of American companies to rely on discounted cash flow techniques in weighing long-term investments.[1] These critics argue that DCF techniques have inherent weaknesses that make them inappropriate for evaluating projects whose payoffs will come years down the road.

We disagree with the contention that DCF techniques are inappropriate for evaluating long-term or strategic investment proposals. We do believe, however, that companies often misapply or misinterpret DCF techniques. Misuse is particularly serious in evaluating long-term capital investments, such as ambitious R&D projects, that appear to involve high risk.

Misapplication of DCF techniques can certainly contribute to an unwarranted aversion to making long-term investments. However, the problem lies not in the technique but in its misuse. Money has a time value in every economy, and cash is the lifeblood of every business. To evaluate cash flows (costs or revenues) generated in different periods requires a procedure for making comparisons. For evaluating and ranking investment proposals, whether they have short or long lives, and involve capital equipment, R&D, or marketing expenditures, we need techniques that recognize that cash flows occur at different times. Discounting provides a rational and conceptually sound procedure for making such evaluations.

---

1 See, for example, Robert H. Hayes and David A. Garvin, "Managing as if Tomorrow Mattered," HBR May–June 1982, p. 71.

Unfortunately DCF techniques, like computers, can yield impressive-looking but misleading outputs when the inputs are flawed. Managers with biased assumptions may end up with biased conclusions. The fault, however, lies not with the technique but with the analyst. The path to improved capital budgeting requires education in the proper use of rational techniques rather than their rejection out of hand.

In our view, DCF techniques provide valuable information to *assist* management in making sound investment decisions. We emphasize the word assist because it is people, rather than analytical tools, who make decisions. Managers may have many objectives and face many constraints in their decision making. Nevertheless, they need information on the relative financial merits of different options. Properly employed, DCF techniques provide such information. The alternative is to ignore the time value of money and implicitly assume that, for example, a dollar earned ten years from now will have the same value as a dollar today.

DCF procedures, as commonly applied, are subject to three serious pitfalls:

Improper treatment of inflation effects, particularly in long-lived projects.

Excessive risk adjustments, particularly when risk declines in later phases of a project.

Failure to acknowledge how management can reduce project risk by diversification and other responses to future events.

Awareness of these pitfalls should help managers avoid uncritical use of DCF techniques that may lead to poor decisions.

An R&D project, for example

Although the comments here apply to a variety of investment proposals, we shall illustrate these three major pitfalls with the analysis of an R&D project. (*Exhibit I* lists examples of other investment projects that are frequently misevaluated for the reasons described in this article.) Because of their risk characteristics, R&D projects present some especially thorny problems. The pronounced uncertainties in these projects affect the analysis of risk in many ways.

Exhibit I	Long-term risky investments frequently misevaluated
1	A consumer goods company considers test marketing the first of a proposed new family of products.
2	A paper company studies investment in a new processing technique that could revolutionize paper making.
3	A drug company looks at increasing its investment in biomedical research and the pilot plant that will be required if the research is successful.
4	A real estate developer analyzes the first-stage investment in improvements at a greenfield site for industrial-commercial facilities.
5	A financial services firm considers investment in a telecommunications facility that could radically alter the future distribution of its services.
6	A natural resources company evaluates a mineral-rights lease of a site that will require extensive development.

As a result, R&D projects with acceptable – even exciting – risk/return profiles may fail to meet the payoff criteria that management has established.

Let's look at a typical (hypothetical) project that would be rejected on the basis of the incomplete DCF analysis common in industry today. Then we'll show how a more complete and careful analysis reveals the project to be not only acceptable but highly desirable.

Our project has three distinct phases, as shown in *Exhibit II*. If the research (Phase 1) is successful, the project moves to market development (Phase 2), after which the resulting product may enjoy a long and profitable period of production and sales. The research and market development phases are periods of investment; returns are forthcoming only during the third period (Phase 3) when the product is sold.

It is important to differentiate between these phases, since each has decidedly different risk characteristics. Market development (Phase 2) will not be undertaken unless the research (Phase 1) is successful; thus, considerable uncertainty disappears before Phase 2 proceeds. Similarly, the sales period (Phase 3) follows only after successful results from research and market development. The information from Phase 2 will refine market projections, and Phase 3 cash flows are relatively low risk. In sum, uncertainty about the project diminishes progressively as we acquire more information.

According to the probabilities shown in *Exhibit II*, the project viewed as a whole (rather than by phases) has the expected-value cash flows shown in *Exhibit III* and an expected internal rate of return (IRR) slightly over 10%. This appears distinctly unattractive, even ridiculous, when compared with customary rates of return (hurdle rates) of 20% or more for high-risk projects. Given this analysis and results, most managers would almost certainly reject the project unless other strategic reasons dictated the investment.

of probabilities and discounting, but it is incomplete and seriously misleading.

Exhibit II	Project description

Phase 1	Research or product development
	$ 18 million annual research cost for 2 years
	60 % probability of success
Phase 2	**Market development**
	Undertaken only if product development succeeds
	$ 10 million annual expenditure for 2 years on the development of marketing and the establishment of marketing and distribution channels (net of any revenues earned in test marketing)
Phase 3	**Sales**
	Proceeds only if Phase 1 and Phase 2 verify opportunity
	Production is subcontracted
	The results of Phase 2 (available at the end of year 4) identify the product's market potential as shown below:

Product demand	Product life	Annual net cash inflow	Probability
High	20 years	$ 24 million	.3
Medium	10 years	$ 12 million	.5
Low	Abandon project	None	.2

Note:
For simplicity, we assume that production is subcontracted in Phase 3 and that all cash flows are after tax and occur at year end. This assumption permits us to ignore some potentially complex tax issues involving depreciation and financing strategies. While a radical departure from reality, this assumption allows us to focus on issues of cash flow timing and risk that appear to be less widely understood.

Exhibit III	Expected cash flows for the project in $ millions

Years	Expected value calculations	
1		−18
2		−18
3	.6 (−10)	= −6
4	.6 (−10)	= −6
5-14	.6 (.3 x 24 + .5 x 12)	=7.92
15-24	.6 (.3 x 24)	=4.32
Expected IRR = 10.1 %		

Many (if not most) U.S. companies, unfortunately, would probably analyze the project in this way, concluding that it is indeed risky and has an expected IRR below normal hurdle rates. The interpretation of these "facts" is far from obvious, however, and requires a deeper understanding of DCF calculation procedures. The issue is not which buttons to push on a calculator, but rather the appropriate interpretation of the inputs and consequent output since the DCF procedure is no more than a processing technique. The analysis appears sophisticated with its use

Adjusting for inflation

The most obvious shortcoming of the analysis is that it ignores how inflation will affect the various cash flows. At one extreme, they may not be affected at all. On the other hand, the cash flows may adjust directly and completely with inflation, that is, an 8% inflation rate next year will raise cash flows in that and following years by 8%. Most likely, inflation will affect different components of the cash flows in different ways and, when aggregated, the cash flows will adjust partially with inflation. Meaningful interpretation of the calculated IRR requires knowledge of this inflation adjustment pattern.

If complete adjustment were anticipated, the calculated IRR would represent an expected real return. However, comparing such real returns with nominal hurdle rates – including inflation – or nominal investment yields (for example, from government bonds) is not appropriate.[2] Historically, real yields on low-risk investments have averaged less than 5%, and the real yield on short-term U.S. Treasury securities has equalled close to zero. For higher risk investments, a frequent standard of comparison is the return (including dividends) on the Standard & Poor's "500" stock index. Over a 53-year period (1926-1978) the real rate of return on the S&P "500" averaged 8.5%. While we cannot be certain that history will repeat itself, long-run averages do provide one standard for comparison. Since listed securities represent an alternative investment, projects of comparable risk reasonably should have expected returns at least as great.

Returning to our hypothetical project, if cash flows adjust fully with inflation, the project offers a real return greater than the historic 8.5% of the S&P "500."

Many types of cash flows, of course, do not adjust fully with inflation, and some do not adjust at all. For example, depreciation tax shields, many lease payments, fixed-rate borrowing (like debentures), and multiyear fixed-price purchase or sales contracts do not change with the inflation rate. Consequently, a proper analysis requires an understanding of the inflation adjustment patterns for different cash flow segments.

2 James C. Van Horne, "A Note on Biases in Capital Budgeting Introduced by Inflation," *Journal of Financial and Quantitative Analysis,* January 1971, p. 653.

While American managers' awareness of the impact of inflation on project evaluation has risen in the last decade, even today many of them have at best a cursory understanding of it. Failure to incorporate inflation assumptions in DCF analyses can be particularly troublesome in decentralized companies. Corporate financial officers commonly specify companywide or divisional hurdle rates based on a current (nominal) cost of capital. Furthermore, analysts at the plant or division level often estimate future cash flows (particularly cost savings) based on current experience. Unless those analysts consciously include anticipated inflation, they will underestimate future cash flows and, unfortunately, many good projects may be rejected.

Parenthetically, the converse is unlikely to occur: it is hard to conceive of an analyst using inflated cash flows with real discount or hurdle rates. Also, projects that go forward usually undergo several reviews that are likely to result in some tempering, or lowering, of overly optimistic cash flow assumptions. By contrast, rejected projects are seldom given subsequent reviews that might reveal unrealistically low inflation assumptions.

The mismatch of inflation assumptions regarding cash flows and hurdle rates is generally most pronounced for projects with payoffs years down the road. So long as the inflation rate is positive (even if declining), the gap between projected real cash flows and their nominal equivalents grows with time. For example, suppose that inflation rates for the next three years are expected to be 8, 6, and 4% respectively. Consider an item that sells for $1 now. If its price will increase at the rate of inflation, its nominal price should be $1.08 next year, $1(1.08)(1.06) = $1.14 in two years, and $1(1.08)(1.06)(1.04) = $1.19 in three years. These inflated prices, rather than the current $1 price, should be incorporated into the DCF analysis if discounting is to occur at nominal rather than real interest rates.

The error that arises from the failure to include inflation in cash flow estimates compounds with time as long as inflation is positive. Under these circumstances, distant cash flows, such as those characteristic of research and development investments, have present values that are more seriously understated. It is difficult to know how widespread such errors have been during recent years, but almost surely they explain in part the shift toward shorter lived projects and myopic investment decisions in many businesses.

Avoiding excessive risk adjustments

A second flaw in the original DCF calculations for our hypothetical R&D project is the use of a single discount rate (IRR) for a project in which risk declines dramatically over time. As a result, the project appears less attractive than it really is. If we make appropriate adjustments for the differing risks in different stages of the project, the investment becomes much more attractive.

A typical discount rate (k) used in DCF analyses may be viewed as composed of three parts: a risk-free time value of money (RF), a premium for expected inflation (Eπ), and a risk premium (Δ) that increases with project risk. This relationship can be represented as:

$$1 + k = (1 + RF) (1 + E\pi) (1 + \Delta)$$

For example, a risk-free rate of 3% with 10% expected inflation and a 6% risk premium would imply $1 + k = (1.03)(1.10)(1.06) = 1.20$, or a nominal discount rate of approximately 20%.

Since inflation, as well as project risk and even the risk-free rate (RF), can vary over time, we should permit k to have different values at different times. The subscript t indicates the relevant time period; thus k_t is a function of the RF_t, $E\pi_t$, and Δ_t values for that period. To focus on situations where project risk is expected to change significantly through time, we will use real (deflated) cash flows and real discount rates with RF constant. It is, of course, very important to adjust for expected inflation properly. Without losing sight of that point, let's shift the focus of discussion to risk adjustments by assuming that the inflation adjustments have been executed properly.

Denoting the real (risky) discount rate for period t as r_t, we have:

$$1 + r_t = (1 + RF) (1 + \Delta_t)$$

This differs from k_t simply by the removal of the inflation factor $(1 + E\pi_t)$. Then by definition, the NPV of a project with expected real cash flows (CF_t) occurring in two periods is:

$$NPV = \frac{CF_1}{1 + r_1} + \frac{CF_2}{(1 + r_1)(1 + r_2)}$$

$$= \frac{CF_1}{(1 + RF)(1 + \Delta_1)}$$

$$+ \frac{CF_2}{(1 + RF)^2 (1 + \Delta_1)(1 + \Delta_2)}$$

This brings us to a key point. If $\Delta_1 = \Delta_2 = \Delta$, this formula collapses into the familiar form with a single discount rate:

$$NPV = \frac{CF_1}{(1 + RF)(1 + \Delta)} + \frac{CF_2}{(1 + RF)^2(1 + \Delta)^2}$$

$$= \frac{CF_1}{1 + r} + \frac{CF_2}{(1 + r)^2}$$

In practice, virtually all DCF calculations are performed using a constant discount rate such as r. Indeed, financial calculators are programmed that way. Under what conditions, however, can we assume that $\Delta_1 = \Delta_2$ (even approximately)?

This assumption is reasonable if we anticipate that errors in predicting real cash flows result from a random walk process – that is, predictions one period into the future always entail the same uncertainty. Thus if we were at time 1, each dollar of real cash flow in period 2 would look just as risky as each dollar of CF_1 looks now. However, predicting two periods into the future is more risky; thus CF_2 viewed from the present deserves a larger risk adjustment. Consequently, CF_2 is multiplied by $1/(1 + \Delta)^2$ as opposed to simply $1/(1 + \Delta)$ for CF_1. In more general terms, the risk adjustment factor for a cash flow t period in the future is $1/(1 + \Delta)^t$. The risk adjustment grows geometrically with time.

Using a single risk-adjusted discount rate, therefore, implies an important and somewhat special assumption about the risks associated with future cash flow estimates: such risks increase geometrically with chronological distance from the present. On the infrequent occasions when this assumption is mentioned, it is usually justified on the grounds that the accuracy of our foresight decreases with time. While that argument has merit, consider what can happen when an investment proposal does not fit this pattern.

Recall our R&D project. If the cash flows of *Exhibit II* are in real terms, the project has an expected real IRR of 10%; but there is a 40% chance of investing $36 million (real, after tax, but undiscounted) during the first two years and receiving nothing. Many decision makers would demand a much higher return than 10% (real or otherwise) to undertake such an investment. If the project proceeds to Phase 3, the cash flows in that phase are considered relatively low risk. The large risk adjustments that were appropriate for early phases are no longer appropriate once we reach Phase 3.

To highlight this point, let's suppose that Phase 3 could be sold if the project successfully proceeds through the first two phases. Given its low risk, potential investors might evaluate Phase 3 with a low discount rate such as 5% (real). Suppose market research reveals a high demand for the product during

Phase 3: 20-year life with annual net cash inflows of $24 million. Discounting these flows at 5%, we reach a value at the beginning of Phase 3 (end of year 4) of $299 million. Thus if strong demand develops for the product, it's possible the rights to produce and market it could be sold for a considerable sum. This value depends, however, on the marketing results from Phase 2. Thus we need to check what happens if less favorable demand conditions are revealed in Phase 2. Performing similar calculations for the other possible market conditions, we obtain the values in *Exhibit IV.*

Even though there is a 20% chance of low demand, the overall expected value of selling Phase 3 is $136 million. Suppose we now recalculate the project's expected IRR assuming such an outright sale of Phase 3 for its expected value: $136 million. Using the 60% probability of Phase 1 success, we calculate the expected cash flows to be those in *Exhibit V.* Those net expected cash flows are equivalent to an expected IRR of approximately 28%. In other words, the prospect that Phase 3 could be sold as just discussed leads us to revise the overall expected IRR for investing in the project from 10 up to 28%. Since these calculations are in real terms, the project now appears quite attractive.

Pushing this analysis one step further, let's assume the project could also be sold at the end of Phase 1 if the research is successful. That is, the new owner after purchasing the project would pay an estimated $10 million per year of Phase 2 costs and receive the Phase 3 value (depending on marketing research results) as shown in *Exhibit IV.* The purchaser would now encounter the expected cash flows indicated in *Exhibit VI.*

Clearly this proposition is riskier than just buying Phase 3, since the marketing research results of Phase 2 are not yet known. Suppose a potential purchaser evaluated the cash flows in *Exhibit VI* using a 20% discount rate (well over twice the historic real return on the S&P "500"). The implied purchase price (present value at the beginning of Phase 2) is slightly over $79 million. But what is the implied return to the first owner – the initial developer of the product who undertakes the risky proposition of investing $18 million for each of two years in research – if a successful project could be sold at the end of two years for $79 million? The expected real return (including the 40% chance of Phase 1 failure) is over 63% – a far cry from our initial estimate.

This analysis illustrates a pitfall in evaluating projects with risk patterns that differ significantly from the simple random walk assumption. In our example, uncertainty is greatest during the first two years. But it is unreasonable to penalize more than 20 years of subsequent cash flows for that risk. To dramatize this point, we have assumed that the project can be sold in its latter phases. Indeed, the project acquires a dramatically high value if Phase 1 succeeds – a point missed by the initial IRR calculation, which implicitly discounted all cash flows at the same rate.

The difficulty with using a single risk-adjusted discount rate (or IRR) is that the analysis blends time discount and risk adjustment factors. Unless project risk follows a simple random walk pattern, this blending is inappropriate. Although this problem is discussed in the academic literature,[3] it is generally ignored in practice. For projects with dramatically different risk phases, the result can be a serious misestimation of project value.

A more appropriate procedure for evaluating such projects is to separate timing and risk adjustments using the concept of certainty equivalent value (CEV). The CEV of a cash flow in a given year is simply its risk-adjusted value in that year. If we converted all future cash flows to CEVs, we could then discount the CEVs to the present using a single risk-free discount rate. With the timing and risk adjustments thus separated, we avoid the possibility of compounding risk adjustments unintentionally.

As a practical matter, attempting to convert each year's cash flow into a CEV can be cumbersome since the CEV for period t may depend on probabilities for cash flows in the previous period (t-1), which in turn depend on probabilities from t-2, and so on. In our example, the cash flows in Phase 3 depend on results from Phases 1 and 2. Indeed, we have assumed that management would abandon the project altogether if the research is unsuccessful or market tests indicate low demand.

Although it is important to consider interactions among cash flows in different periods, the analysis of all possible management responses or other contingencies would be extraordinarily complex and unwieldy. Thus we need reasonable approximations. Managers and analysts must exercise judgment regarding which risks and possible actions should be included in the analysis. We recommend that high-risk projects be evaluated as a sequence of distinct risk phases (of perhaps several years each).

In our example, we did not attempt to calculate CEVs for each year in Phase 3. Rather, we estimated a value for the whole phase conditional on the demand level. Similarly, our calculated $79 million value for the project if Phase 1 succeeded is a CEV (at the beginning of year three) for Phases 2 and 3 combined. In both cases, these CEVs are estimates of the project's potential selling price – its market value at the end of years two and four respectively. While the project might be worth more to the company if it retained all phases, the market CEVs represent opportunity

3 See, for example, Alexander A. Robichek and Stewart C. Myers, "Conceptual Problems in the Use of Risk-Adjusted Discount Rates," *Journal of Finance*, December 1966, p. 727.

Exhibit IV **Anticipated Phase 3 values if sold**
in $ millions

Demand	Probability	Value of Phase 3 year 4
High	.3	299
Medium	.5	93
Low	.2	0
Expected value =		136

Exhibit V **Expected cash flows with Phase 3 sale**
in $ millions

Year	Outflow	Inflow	Net
1	−18		− 18
2	−18		− 18
3	−10 x .6		− 6
4	−10 x .6	136 x .6	75.6

Exhibit VI **Expected cash flows for purchaser of Phase 2**
in $ millions

Year	Outflow	Inflow	Net
3	−10		− 10
4	−10	136	126

Exhibit VII **Expected cash flows if the project can be abandoned during Phase 1**
in $ millions

Year	Expected outflow	Expected inflow	Expected net cash flow
1	−18		−18
2	−18 x .8	79 x .6	33

costs for retaining Phases 2 and 3 that are useful (and conservative) yardsticks for evaluating the entire project.

Estimating market values for different phases is obviously an imprecise process. Using a single risk-adjusted rate for an entire phase (rather than separate rates or CEVs for each cash flow) produces only an approximation, unless risks within that phase have a random walk pattern. The approximation is reasonable, however, if the discount rate is low and/or the phase covers a fairly short period of time (as in Phases 1 and 2 above). If a phase is both long and risky, analysts should divide it into subphases.

To restate our argument, we recommend segmenting projects into risk phases, then valuing sequentially each phase, working backward from the last. This procedure can be used to determine either an expected IRR on the initial phase (as already illustrated) or an NPV for the project. In general, we prefer calculating NPVs since this avoids technical problems with IRR, including scale ambiguities. Although slightly more complex than a standard expected NPV or IRR calculation, our approach is not difficult per se. It simply entails a short sequence of expected NPV calculations using different interest rates to value different risk phases. When a project's risk pattern differs substantially from the simple random walk assumption, such differences should be recognized and the evaluation procedure modified accordingly. As we have shown, evaluation based on inappropriate analysis can be very misleading.

Considering the eye of the beholder

A third major problem in project evaluations is correctly assessing project risk and how managers can influence its nature and level. Here it is important to consider the perspective of the analyst. Risk that seems excessive to an R&D or project manager may appear reasonable to a corporate executive or a shareholder who can diversify the risk by spreading it across other investments. Also, managers can influence the level of risk by future actions that affect the ultimate payoff of a project investment.

Frequently, the major uncertainty in R&D investments is whether the research phase will produce a viable product. From the perspective of financial market theories such as the Capital Asset Pricing Model (CAPM), risks associated with the research phase are apt to be largely diversifiable. Consequently, a public shareholder with a well-diversified securities portfolio will probably voice little or no concern about these risks. Success or failure in the lab is probably correlated weakly (if at all) with broad economic forces or other systematic nondiversifiable factors that affect returns in the stock market as a whole.

The CAPM and related theories stress that a project's total risk normally contains both diversifiable and nondiversifiable components. To the extent shareholders can easily diversify their holdings in the financial markets, they can reduce *their* portion of the project's diversifiable risk to a very small level. Under these circumstances, the shareholders need worry only about the systematic portion of project risk. Thus a financial market approach suggests that the typical R&D project is much less risky from the perspective of a well-diversified public shareholder

Calculating inflation's effects

To correctly allow for inflation in a DCF analysis, some analysts include it in the cash flows and use nominal discount rates. If inflation rates are expected to vary, different discount rates can be used for different years in a net present value (NPV) calculation. Such a procedure, however, entails cumbersome calculations. Furthermore, consistency on a companywide basis requires specifying the annual series of discount and inflation rates to be used by analysts. The simple approach is to use a single "average" inflation rate with a single nominal discount rate, but this is not ideal. Although in many cases the distortion associated with this approximation is not serious, the pattern of cash flows and projected inflation affects the size of the distortion.

A preferable procedure is to use deflated cash flows with real discount rates. In this approach, analysts estimate the cash flow in each period, including the increase from inflation applicable to each of its segments (for example, zero for depreciation tax shields). Analysts then deflate the cash flow to present (for example, 1985) dollars using the projected inflation between now and that period. If the cash flow is expected to adjust fully with inflation, the deflation adjustment will exactly cancel the included inflation. If not, the real value of that future cash flow will be altered by the extent to which it does not fully adjust with inflation. The series of deflated (real) cash flows can then be discounted using real discount rates. Since the real time value of money appears to be considerably more stable than its nominal counterpart, this second procedure is superior to using a single nominal discount rate.

than it may appear to the individual performing the DCF analysis.

In contrast, managers, creditors, and even suppliers may focus on total risk (including both diversifiable and systematic components) at the company level. These groups have interests that are not easily diversified in the sense that the CAPM assumes. Thus they are concerned about total cash flow variability but at the company (not project) level. Even at the company level, however, the R&D budget may be spread across many projects. A multi-industry company of even moderate size is probably sufficiently diversified to allow large reductions in cash flow variability per dollar of R&D investment. Once again, the risk of a particular project appears lower from a portfolio perspective than from the perspective of an analyst looking only at the project itself.

Most managers are aware of portfolio effects and the arguments regarding shareholder welfare based on financial market models such as the CAPM. Nevertheless, it is understandable that they view a project with over a 50% chance of no payoff (as in our example) as highly risky. Under such circumstances, it is easy to ignore portfolio effects and worry too much about the risk of that particular investment opportunity. This excessive risk aversion is frequently manifested in a too-high discount or hurdle rate, thus compounding the pitfalls already discussed.

Analysts may also use conservative estimates: overestimates of development time or costs and underestimates of both the magnitude and duration of subsequent payoffs. Although the tendency toward excessive conservatism is both inevitable and difficult to overcome, management needs to be aware of its existence and sensitive to its consequences. As we said earlier, projects that have been rejected are seldom reevaluated. It is all too easy for a good project to be lost.

While excessive risk adjustments are certainly not unique to R&D proposals, the problem may be more severe here because R&D projects involve large and obvious uncertainties. The key is that these risks are likely to be highly diversifiable. Failure to recognize this fact represents a systematic bias against R&D projects.

Managers can also affect the level of risk by influencing the distribution of project payoffs. In our example, there is a 30% chance that Phase 3 will be worth $299 million. There is not a symmetric chance of losing $299 million – because the company will abandon the project if faced with low product demand. The result is an *expected* value for Phase 3 ($136 million) which is $43 million above the *most likely* estimate of $93 million. Unfortunately, many project evaluations consider only the most likely cash flow estimates and ignore the asymmetry or skewness of the payoffs. This practice understates the project's true value in situations in which future management actions can improve profits or limit losses.

This problem is more significant for R&D projects than for other investments because the company has greater flexibility to expand production for highly successful products and to abandon apparently unprofitable efforts. Such managerial actions can result in greater returns than estimated originally (larger revenues over a longer period) as well as reduced downside risk.

In our example, suppose progress can be monitored throughout Phase 1, and management has the option to abandon the project at the end of the first year if certain goals are not met. If the probability of research failure is equally divided between years one and two (20% each), the expected IRR from an initial investment in Period 1 research increases from 63% to 83%, with no change in our other assumptions (*Exhibit VII* shows the relevant cash flows). Clearly management's ability to skew a payoff distribution in the company's favor can have an important influence on a project's desirability.

DCF analysis in perspective

How much the misuse of DCF techniques has contributed to the competitive troubles of American companies is a matter of conjecture. It is clear, though, that incomplete analysis can severely penalize investments whose payoffs are both uncertain and far in the future. Given these perils, one might argue that DCF procedures should be avoided or should be accorded little weight in long-term investment decisions. We strongly disagree. It is foolish to ignore or to indict useful analytical tools simply because they might be used incorrectly or incompletely. Rather, analysts and decision makers should recognize potential problems and be careful to ensure that evaluations are performed correctly. Managers cannot treat a DCF evaluation like a black box, looking only at the output. They need to break open the box, examine the assumptions inside, and determine how those assumptions affect the analysis of a project's long-term profitability.

DCF procedures can help evaluate the implications of altered price, cost, or timing assumptions, but managers must first specify the correct assumptions. These procedures can also be used to examine the effects of different capacity expansion or R&D strategies under many scenarios. However, again managers must specify the strategies or scenarios to be examined. In short, discounting is only one step in evaluating alternative investment opportunities. This fact has frequently been lost in the arguments (pro and con) about the use of discounting procedures.

Blaming DCF procedures for shortsightedness, biased perceptions, excessive risk aversion, or other alleged management weaknesses does not address the underlying problems of American industry. However, understanding the pitfalls in the casual use of DCF techniques can both improve the analysis of capital investment projects and place these techniques in a more appropriate perspective.

It is important to remember that managers make decisions. DCF techniques can assist in that process, but they are only tools. Correctly used, these techniques provide a logical and consistent framework for comparing cash flows occurring at different times – an important aspect of virtually every investment project. ⊽

Reprint 85106

Assessing capital risk: you can't be too conservative

Jasper H. Arnold III

*"Worst case forecasts
are almost always too optimistic."*

In the summer of 1981, the top officers of the Cloud Tool Company, a large oil-field equipment manufacturer, were nervous about borrowing $15 million from their bank to finance a large plant expansion. They had chosen this investment over several smaller ones because it would enable the company to hold onto, or even raise, its share of the rapidly growing, and continually profitable, energy market. To ensure that the company was not assuming too much risk, the financial staff did a worst case forecast. The forecast showed that—even under adverse circumstances—the company had enough cash to repay the debt.

By late 1982, management nervousness had turned to fear. The oil business had fallen into a severe recession, the company had reported large losses, and cash generation had dropped. A principal payment on the bank loan was due at the end of the year, and the finance VP had projected that the company would not have enough cash on hand. A default would mean that the bank could foreclose on the pledged assets or force an involuntary bankruptcy. Only then did the managers realize that their worst case scenario had been much too optimistic. If they had opted for a more modest expansion, the existence of their company probably would not be in jeopardy.

Many managers don't realize that when they finance a large expansion project with debt, they may be assuming far too much risk. High profit potential, personal commitment to the project, or faith in the industry can hamper executives' vision of the future. They want it to be rosy, so they avoid acknowledging that a crisis could occur. But if the project incurs large

Jasper Arnold is a senior vice president and manager of the credit department at First City National Bank of Houston. This is his second article for HBR. His first, "How to Negotiate a Term Loan," appeared in March-April 1982.

losses, the company's financial resources and flexibility can waste away. At the extreme, the company can fail. A critical part of capital budgeting should be a realistic—and conservative—worst case analysis.

When a company gets into trouble, lending banks do a staying power analysis. It is a conservative way to assess the company resources available to repay loans under distressed circumstances. To see how well their company could withstand financial setbacks, managers can also use this method before embarking on a capital expansion program. Then if they want to bet the company, at least they know that's what they're doing.

As a banker at a large New York bank and now at a regional bank in Texas, I have been involved in the financing of many capital expenditure programs. I have also turned down requests. In every case, I have heard management justify the investment and have seen the supporting analysis. Over time, I have seen the outcomes of their decisions. These experiences have taught me that:

Most large capital expenditure programs encounter large problems.

These problems can be financially destructive if the company has invested on too grand a scale.

Without a realistic worst case scenario, managers often don't appreciate the amount of risk their companies assume.

Staying power analysis helps managers both evaluate worst case performance and decide on a project's size.

When undertaking a large expansion program, management usually acknowledges that it might face some short-term reversals or minor problems, but it generally is convinced that nothing serious will happen and that the project will succeed. This optimism is unjustified. In fact, most projects—more than 50% by my estimate—encounter big setbacks. A Rand Corporation study found that the first construction-cost estimate of process plants involving new technology was usually less than half of the final cost, and many projects experience even worse performance. Research using PIMS data revealed that more than 80% of the new projects studied failed to achieve their market-share targets.[1]

My experience and discussions with other bankers and executives show that in at least one out of five projects, managers regret their investments because of large or persistent losses. An aircraft manufacturer, for example, undertook production of a new commercial jetliner. Its major subcontractor went bankrupt, and there was insufficient demand for the jetliner. The company suffered large losses and eventually had to terminate production. I have seen examples like this in the defense contracting, chemical, and microcomputer industries as well.

When worst cases look too good

Today's complex and treacherous business environment raises the chance that a company will encounter trouble. My experience in the last decade with companies in the energy industry motivated me, in large part, to write this article. What occurred there vividly illustrates the business environment's instability and the difficulties this creates in capital budgeting.

After the Arab oil embargo of 1973, the oil business enjoyed the strongest boom in its history. It lasted until the end of 1981 when the posted price of OPEC crude peaked at $34 per barrel. Companies made tremendous investments aimed at finding more oil and gas, and they financed many of these investments with debt. Some companies did implement smaller capital expenditure programs, but many leaned toward large, ambitious projects because of the tantalizing profits and the seemingly permanent nature of the boom.

In early 1982, the bubble burst. Because of the worldwide glut of oil and natural gas, OPEC had

to cut prices. The oil companies reduced their exploration activity, and a cataclysmic decline in profits ensued. A large number of companies went bankrupt, and many still teeter on the brink with cash flows barely above the level required to service debt.

The severely troubled energy companies share a common experience: management made capital expenditures that were far too large for the company's size, and it financed them with debt. When earnings are strong, companies may be able to service a large amount of debt, but when business activity and cash flow drop, principal and interest payments can be so large that the company cannot operate for long without defaulting on a loan. Under these circumstances, companies have little time to cut expenses or sell assets to generate cash, and lenders are usually unwilling to advance additional funds to companies they already view as too highly leveraged.

Cloud Tool Company's story is fairly typical. Its top management ignored a business tenet: the bigger the project, the more money it will lose if it gets in trouble. To make large capital expenditures, a business must be able to sustain large losses, either through earnings from other products or, if the company is undiversified, through a large equity base that can absorb the losses and still comfort the lenders by protecting their loans.

Unfortunately, the oil industry's experience is not unusual. The sky has fallen on many industries—textile manufacturing, chemical production, cement manufacturing, commercial real estate development, and home computer manufacturing—just when managers thought they had found the pot of gold at the end of the rainbow. Unstable energy cartels, rapid technological change, deregulation of protected industries, aggressive foreign competition, industry recessions, and legions of professional managers who are well schooled in exploiting their companies' strengths and attacking their competitors' weaknesses contribute to this uncertainty.

Most companies support large capital expenditure programs with a worst case analysis that examines the project's loss potential. But the worst case forecast is almost always too optimistic. When problems occur, the financial results are usually much worse than the predictions. When managers look at the downside, they generally describe a mildly pessimistic future rather than the worst possible future.

A worst case analysis conventionally entails preparing a pessimistic cash flow forecast to determine if operations can generate enough cash to repay debt according to its contractual terms. But this approach has some problems. First, a very pessimistic analysis often reveals that the company cannot service the debt at all, especially if the project is large for the company's size. This unhappy result tends to bias the forecaster toward only mild pessimism when divining the future. Second, cash flow from operations is not necessarily the only source of cash for debt repayment during hard times; lenders will sometimes make additional loans or defer payments on existing debt. Finally, this approach does not indicate the costs of such lender assistance because it is not conducted from a lender's standpoint.

Staying power analysis is a better way to do a worst case forecast. When a borrower gets into financial trouble, bankers employ this technique to see how much additional money they can advance to cover cash deficits or if it would be prudent to defer principal payments until the company's health improves. Management can use staying power analysis to determine if the company can avoid a default on loans or other obligations and thereby avoid an involuntary bankruptcy, a lawsuit for payment, or a foreclosure on pledged assets. The technique can also help managers decide on the appropriate size of an important capital expenditure.

Lender's perspective

To conduct a staying power analysis, a manager must understand the lender's viewpoint. A cardinal rule of credit is to have two sources of repayment. The primary source of repayment is always the business's operating cash flow. If the most likely forecast shows that this source is inadequate, the lender will usually not make the loan. The secondary source of repayment is the liquidation value of assets; it comes into play when the company gets into trouble and can only generate a very low – or negative – cash flow.

If a company actually begins to show losses, however, and can't service debt from internal sources, lenders do not like to liquidate assets. Liquidation values are uncertain, and a forced bankruptcy or foreclosure is expensive and time-consuming and may tarnish the lender's competitive image. Lenders would rather work with management to keep the company alive so that repayment can ultimately come from cash generation. Such accommodations, however, are by no means automatic and may be costly. Lenders must have confidence in management's ability and must believe that the company has a good chance of returning to profitability. They must believe that the liquidation value of the assets representing their collateral is, or soon will be, equal to or greater than their outstanding loans. If asset coverage is inadequate, lenders are prone to move immediately against the assets before more losses further reduce their value.

The borrowing base is the maximum loan value that lenders ascribe to the company's assets. It is critical to staying power analysis. Here are some fairly representative borrowing-base values of assets normally considered acceptable collateral: accounts receivable are worth 80% of carrying value; inventory is worth 50% of carrying value; and land, buildings, and equipment are worth 90% of "orderly liquidation value" (the amount that could be realized in a piecemeal sale of the assets after a diligent search for interested buyers and an effort at negotiating a favorable price).

Accounts receivable must be fairly current and owed by financially sound companies. The type of inventory affects the amount of credit it will support. Commodity raw materials, such as petrochemical resins or steel scrap, have a readily determined market value and can be assigned a fairly high advance rate – usually 60% to 75% of cost. Finished goods such as consumer durables, where style is not a factor, or standard steel shapes may be similarly treated. Specialty raw materials or finished goods with a narrow market will have only a 25% to 50% advance rate. Work-in-process inventory rarely has any borrowing value.

Lenders frequently use outside appraisers to value fixed assets. In times of distress, lenders will usually advance 80% to 90% of orderly liquidation value. For analysis purposes, these values should be very low for special-purpose equipment or for large, special-purpose manufacturing plants that would have a limited resale value if an industry got into serious trouble or if a new manufacturing technology failed. Twenty-five to thirty cents on the cost dollar is not unreasonable. Your banker will confirm that such assets have sold for less.

"While you were out! Let's see. Oh, yes. Everybody in the office plunged into a state of despondency and funk, pending your return."

Analyze staying power

To illustrate how staying power analysis works, I will use the example of Acme Fabrication Company, an industrial product manufacturer. It reported 1985 sales of $35.1 million and net profits of $1.9 million. In early 1986, management was considering making a large addition to its plant that it hoped would dramatically raise sales. If it made the addition immediately, the cost of the fixed assets would be $12 million. The company could arrange financing in the form of a five-year bank term loan to be repaid in equal annual installments of principal.

Management also had the option of making the investment in phases: $6.5 million in 1986 and then, if things went as expected, another $6.8 million in 1987. Note that for the same amount of capacity the phased expansion was more expensive than the immediate, large investment: $13.3 million versus $12 million. This was because of inflation over two years and the cost economies in constructing and equipping the large-scale project. Another unattractive feature of the phased approach was the prospect of lower sales and earnings over the life of the project relative to the results of the large-scale option because by spending the money in increments the company could not achieve certain production and marketing economies.

The same bank would provide all existing and new debt, and the loans would initially be unsecured. The company had a $6.5 million line of credit at this bank and $3.9 million was outstanding in the form of notes payable.

Both options were analyzed from a strategic standpoint and were found acceptable. The company also used discounted cash flow hurdles, and both alternatives met the minimum standard.

Describe a hostile environment. Begin the staying power analysis by forecasting the financial performance that would result from the most hostile environment that might *reasonably* occur. I emphasize the word "reasonably" because one can paint such a bleak picture that survival is impossible. While not a pleasant task, describing a disaster scenario is fairly simple. For Acme, the chief risks were a steep industry recession and rising steel costs. Since the industry's cyclical swings did not always coincide with the ups and downs of steel prices, management thought that the company might have to contend with rising steel costs during an industrywide recession.

The forecaster then translates the description of the hostile operating environment into financial results. Nearly every risk predictably shows up in a company's financial statements. The impact of the

Exhibit I

Impact of hostile environment on Acme's financial statements

Risks	Impact on financial statements
Steep industry recession	Declining prices due to falling unit sales volume and lower selling prices
	Slow inventory turnover due to excess or hard-to-move stock
	Slow accounts receivable collection period due to the effects of the recession on customers
Rising raw materials costs	Rise in cost of goods sold because of higher steel costs and higher per unit manufacturing costs due to lower production volume

hostile environment on Acme's statements appears in *Exhibit I.*

Estimate erosion potential. Quantifying the duration of the bad period and the dollar magnitudes is the hardest part. With experience or good strategic risk analysis, management can usually estimate the range of outcomes for each affected financial statement account. When making these estimates, focus on each account's erosion potential: the most deterioration that might occur in the hostile operating environment. For some financial statement variables, thinking in absolute terms is convenient: "Accounts receivable collection period could conceivably rise to 120 days in a severe recession." For others, using percentages is handier: "Sales could fall by 30% over two years."

Historical results are a good source of information for estimating erosion potential, but a tranquil past often gives false comfort. In dynamic and evolving markets, the future may present obstacles never encountered before. Managers, therefore, should err on the conservative side and estimate results much worse than those seen in the past. If the worst historical sales performance has been a 25% drop over two years, management might run the forecast based on a 35% drop. In studying historical data, managers should go 10 or 15 years back if possible. They can also gain insights from studying the results of other companies in the industry.

The executives may have trouble admitting that some worst case scenarios are possible, but history shows that they do often happen. Therefore, if the purpose of the expansion is to turn out a new product, assume that unit sales volume is 60% to 85% of the levels your most likely projections assume. The exact discount will depend on the amount of market research and testing done, the competition's ability to retaliate or otherwise preclude you from achieving the anticipated market share, and other factors that might affect the risk of buyer acceptance.

If the purpose of the expansion is to employ new production technology, do what bankers do: run your projections assuming that the project never works and that the company must repay its debt from the base business's cash flows. If you ran a successful pilot plant or implemented other risk-reducing measures, assume large cost overruns and a long delay in reaching commercial production levels.

Don't ignore working capital. Managers without a financial orientation often ignore or drastically underestimate the total amount of money a project ultimately requires. They think in terms of fixed assets—land, building, and equipment—and do not think enough about the additional investment in net working capital. In Acme's case, the large-scale option required a $12 million fixed-asset investment but, as we will see shortly, the amount needed the first year to get the project under way was much more—$19.3 million. The company needed the additional $7.3 million because the new plant caused sales to rise, which led to higher accounts receivable and meant that more inventory had to be carried. A "spontaneous" rise in accounts payable and accrued liabilities automatically supplied part of the financing to support this, but an external source had to fund the balance. For most companies this source is debt, which increases leverage and, therefore, risk.

Include cost-cutting efforts. The forecaster must also anticipate what cash conservation programs the company would implement when financially distressed. Management would probably make these decisions:

Cut selling, general, and administrative (SG & A) expenses.

Sell marketable securities.

Reduce inventory levels.

Cut the dividend.

Reduce capital expenditures.

Sell unnecessary assets.

Delay paying vendors.

The company can only go so far with some of these actions. In preparing financial forecasts, managers often assume that sales drive many balance sheet and income statement accounts. For example, if sales drop by 10%, they assume a 10% decline in accounts receivable, inventory, selling, and general and administrative expenses. But when companies get into trouble this is usually not the case, especially at the onset of financial difficulty. Unsure how severe the situation will get or how long it will last, executives hesitate to reduce inventories or to cut SG&A expenses. And the company's financial condition has to deteriorate dramatically before management will consider firing people.

The same is true about cutting the dividend. Management wants to protect sensitive stockholders and show the stock market that all is well. Capital expenditures may not be easy to reduce either. Equipment-purchase or construction contracts may have been signed months before the problems arose, or the manufacturing process may ruin the equipment so that it must be frequently replaced. So it's best to assume that any big cuts will be delayed and slow to take effect. Moreover, SG&A expenses and capital spending cannot be cut beyond a certain point, and the sales force may be unable to get rid of excessive inventories if the bottom falls out of the market.

One more reality of hard times needs mentioning. I have seen many forecasts in which managers try to reflect a worst case scenario and assume a drop in sales but hold gross margins about in line with historical levels. In most industry recessions, what actually happens is this: declining sales volume stimulates price cutting, and as excess production capacity rises, price cutting becomes rampant as companies try to generate orders that at least cover out-of-pocket costs; as production is reduced to reflect the drop in sales, unit costs rise as fixed costs are spread over fewer units. The impact of this on gross profits is magnified because the falling sales prices and the rising unit costs squeeze the margin on each unit sold, and the company sells fewer units. To make matters worse, the company's customers usually take longer to pay because either they have the power of a buyer's market or they are also hurt by the recession and try to conserve cash.

Acme created its forecasts from these types of assumptions. Based on current backlog and market strength, management thought it reasonable to expect a good year in 1986 followed by a steep, two-year recession with drastically falling sales, shrinking profit margins, and a slowdown in inventory and receivables turnover. The company made the assumption that payables would be stretched and marketable securities sold to generate cash, but that it would delay big cuts in SG&A expenses and capital expenditures until 1988.

Exhibit II shows the staying power analysis for the large-scale project. The top part is the forecast income statement. A $1.5 million loss occurs in 1987 followed by a severe loss of $4.4 million in 1988; thereafter the company returns to profitability.

Exhibit II	**Acme's staying power analysis for a large project** in millions of dollars*						

			Actual	Projected				
			1985	1986	1987	1988	1989	1990
Income statement	**Income and expenses**	Net sales	$ 35.1	$ 61.1	$ 53.0	$ 43.0	$ 53.0	$ 56.0
		Cost of goods sold	24.6	44.5	43.4	39.4	40.9	42.4
		Gross profit	10.5	16.6	9.6	3.6	12.1	13.6
		Selling, general, and administrative expense	5.5	9.6	9.6	9.1	7.6	7.6
		Interest expense	1.5	2.9	2.8	2.6	2.4	2.0
		Profit before tax	3.5	4.1	− 2.8	− 8.1	2.1	4.0
		Income taxes	1.6	1.9	− 1.3	− 3.7	1.0	1.8
		Net income	**1.9**	**2.3**	**− 1.5**	**− 4.4**	**1.1**	**2.2**
Balance sheet	**Assets**	Cash and marketable securities	$ .4	$ .4	$ .3	$ .3	$ .3	$ .3
		Accounts receivable	5.8	10.0	9.1	7.7	9.0	9.2
		Inventory	8.8	15.3	15.0	14.5	14.0	14.5
		Current assets	**15.0**	**25.7**	**24.4**	**22.5**	**23.3**	**24.0**
		Net fixed assets	17.5	26.1	23.7	20.8	17.9	15.0
		Total assets	**32.5**	**51.8**	**48.1**	**43.3**	**41.2**	**39.0**
	Liabilities and stockholders' equity	Accounts payable and accrued liabilities	4.7	8.2	8.4	8.2	8.5	8.9
		Current maturities of long-term debt	1.0	3.4	3.4	3.4	3.4	3.4
		Notes payable (existing)	3.9	3.9	3.9	3.9	3.9	3.9
		Additional short-term debt	−	2.5	3.6	6.7	6.6	5.3
		Current liabilities	**9.6**	**18.0**	**19.3**	**22.2**	**22.4**	**21.5**
		Long-term debt	9.0	17.6	14.2	10.8	7.4	4.0
		Stockholders' equity	13.9	16.2	14.6	10.2	11.4	13.6
		Total liabilities and stockholders' equity	**32.5**	**51.8**	**48.1**	**43.3**	**41.2**	**39.0**
Sources and uses of cash	**Sources**	Net income		$ 2.3	$−1.5	$−4.4	$ 1.1	$ 2.2
		Depreciation		3.4	3.4	3.4	3.4	3.4
		Total sources		**5.7**	**1.9**	**− 1.0**	**4.5**	**5.6**
	Uses	Capital expenditures		12.0	1.0	.5	.5	.5
		Long-term debt repayment		1.0	3.4	3.4	3.4	3.4
		Change in net working capital†		7.3	− 1.5	− 1.7	.5	.4
		Total uses		**20.3**	**2.9**	**2.2**	**4.4**	**4.3**
		Cash flow before external financing (S-U)		−14.6	− 1.0	− 3.2	.1	1.3
		+ New long-term debt or stock		12.0	−	−	−	−
		+ Increase (decrease) in additional short-term debt and notes payable (existing)		2.5	1.0	3.2	− .1	− 1.3
		Change in cash and marketable securities		**− .1**	**0**	**0**	**0**	**0**
Borrowing base analysis		Borrowing base‡		$ 28.7	$ 26.7	$ 23.8	$ 23.2	$ 22.1
		− Required indebtedness§		27.4	25.1	24.8	21.3	16.6
		Excess (deficient) borrowing base		**1.3**	**1.6**	**− 1.0**	**1.9**	**5.5**

*Columns may not add up to totals because of rounding.

†Except cash and marketable securities, notes payable (existing), additional short-term debt, and current maturities of long-term debt.

‡Calculated using year-end balance sheet values: 80% of accounts receivable plus 50% of inventory plus 50% of net fixed assets.

§The total required borrowings at year-end: current maturities of long-term debt plus notes payable (existing) plus additional short-term debt plus long-term debt.

Four questions

Acme's management must now assess the impact of this worst case scenario on the company's solvency. Does the company have enough staying power to get through the bad years of 1987 and 1988 without a creditor-initiated legal action? Four questions must be answered.

Do we need external financing to get through the bad period? The best outcome, of course, would be to generate enough cash from internal sources to service debt and cover the losses during the downturn. Some companies with floundering projects may be able to do this if: (1) the company is not highly leveraged; (2) the project, while large in absolute dollar terms, is small relative to the company's size; or (3) the project's cash flows are inversely correlated with the cash flows of the base business so that if the project goes bad, the base business can still generate enough cash. Under such circumstances, the company does not have to seek external financing or request deferrals of principal payments. This position indicates a high degree of staying power and suggests that the project does not create excessive risk.

The additional short-term debt line on the balance sheet (as shown in *Exhibit II*) tells the story. It is the forecasting "plug number" that makes the balance sheet balance. The number rises when the company operates at a cash flow deficit and must obtain external debt financing. It falls when the company generates surplus cash and repays the debt. In Acme's case, the figure takes a big jump to $2.5 million in 1986, a profitable year, because the company must boost its current assets to support the new sales the plant expansion generates. The company obtains this amount by drawing under its line of credit, which would then be fully used.

Then in 1987 and 1988, the problem years, the company needs $4.2 million more in short-term borrowings because of the losses and the repayment of long-term debt. Thus if the worst case scenario came to pass, Acme would have to get the bank's assistance.

Do lenders have to supply any "net new money"? Banks and other lenders are more willing to work with a troubled borrower if they do not have to raise their risk exposure. Provided that the company has minimal collateral coverage—one dollar of borrowing base for each dollar loaned—they view their existing loans as spilled milk that they hope eventually to recover from cash flow after the borrower has returned to profitability. Under such circumstances, lenders will usually advance funds to make payments on other debts owed to them or, more likely, defer the payments.

But if a forecast shows that, in spite of attempts to conserve cash, the company must still seek net new financing, then the risks may appear too high. Banks and other lenders do not see themselves as suppliers of money to finance losses; equity capital does that. Nor do they like to advance money to a severely troubled company so that it can repay other lenders.

While bankers will occasionally advance limited amounts of new funds, forecasters are foolish to presume that the bank will be willing to raise its loss exposure. The conservative forecaster should not expect to get net new money unless the company has a legally binding revolving credit commitment and the forecast shows that no restrictive covenants would be broken that would permit the bank to cancel the commitment. Draws should be assumed under a nonlegally binding line of credit only during the first year of a problem period because these credits are renewable at yearly intervals at the bank's option. The draws should be covered at least one-to-one by the borrowing base since the bank, which is only morally bound under a line of credit, could refuse the draw requests unless the company has collateral coverage.

Acme borrows from one bank, so even though additional short-term debt rises in 1987 and 1988, the decline in required indebtedness (shown at the bottom of *Exhibit II*) means that the short-term bank loans merely furnish the cash to repay the bank's long-term debt on time. Thus the bank does not have to supply any net new money. In reality, the bank would probably defer the principal payments on the long-term debt. Its willingness to support Acme will depend on Acme's having minimal collateral coverage.

Can the company stay in compliance with its borrowing base? At the bottom of *Exhibit II* is the borrowing base analysis, which shows how much debt Acme's assets will support. The analysis shows that the company lacks the staying power to survive. It would need to incur maximum borrowings (required indebtedness) in 1988 of $24.8 million, but it can only support debt of $23.8 million. Thus if Acme implements the large-scale expansion and encounters very hard times, it could not count on lender support when debts and other obligations come due. Acme could face an involuntary bankruptcy or other legal action. It should, therefore, reject this expansion option as too risky.

What are the costs of lender assistance? Lender assistance may take several forms depending on the situation: loans under existing credit commitments, deferrals of principal payments, or advances of new money outside existing commitments. At the

Exhibit III   **Assessing staying power**

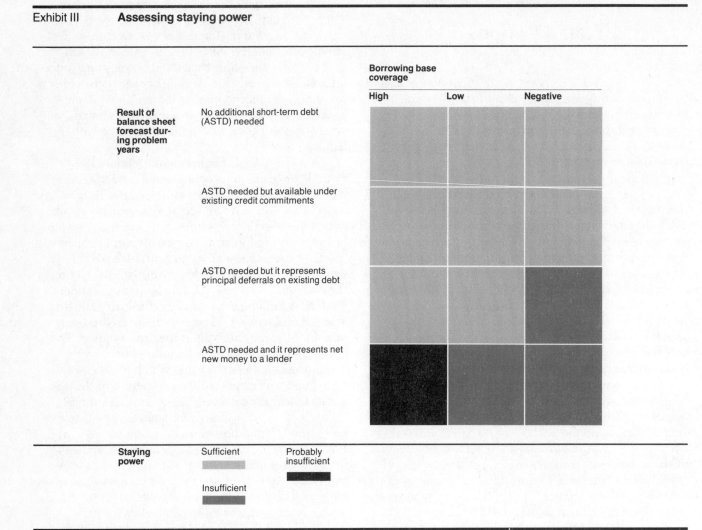

	Borrowing base coverage		
Result of balance sheet forecast during problem years	**High**	**Low**	**Negative**
No additional short-term debt (ASTD) needed			
ASTD needed but available under existing credit commitments			
ASTD needed but it represents principal deferrals on existing debt			
ASTD needed and it represents net new money to a lender			

Staying power   Sufficient   Probably insufficient

Insufficient

least, the costs of this assistance will include tougher loan terms:

A pledge of collateral if loans are unsecured or additional collateral if they are already secured.

Guarantees of repayment by subsidiaries.

The owners' personal guarantees if the company is privately held.

New covenants that tightly control or eliminate various cash drains: dividend payments, capital expenditures, and outside investments.

An interest rate increase.

In addition to these changes in loan terms, as a lender's risk of loss grows, it will usually pressure management or the board of directors to reduce expenses (that is, cut head count) and sell assets to generate cash, seek a buyer for the company, or replace management.

The following guidelines will help managers gauge the costs of lender assistance:

☐   Demands for more stringent loan terms start if company losses persist past three or four quarters, especially if the company violates a restrictive covenant in a loan agreement. But a high borrowing base coverage will postpone or minimize these demands.

☐   Regardless of borrowing base coverage, if losses continue more than two years, lender demands will be heard, and unless coverage is high, the lender will apply some pressure.

☐   If principal deferrals are necessary, expect the full range of demands and expect pressure to be brought to bear. If the borrowing base coverage is low or losses are large, the resulting pressure can be intense.

☐ When the company's committed credit facilities are fully used and it still needs new money, the lender may exert intense pressures and deny the loan requests. Such denials will usually lead to a default on one or more obligations.

Acme did a staying power analysis on phase one of the $6.5 million small-scale expansion. Additional short-term debt would be necessary in 1987 and 1988. Even though earnings were considerably less than in the large-scale option, since less debt had to be repaid, the company had an adequate borrowing base to survive the recession. The total borrowing requirement was $18.6 million in 1988; it was narrowly covered by a borrowing base of $19.5 million. Acme would need additional short-term debt in 1987 and 1988 to repay existing long-term bank debt, that is, a principal deferral. In exchange for this assistance, management should expect intense demands and pressures since the losses would be long lasting and the borrowing base coverage would be low.

The decision

The type of lender assistance, if any, needed during the problem years plus the borrowing base coverage tell whether a capital-spending program would leave the company with enough staying power to avoid creditors calling a default and demanding payment during hard times. *Exhibit III* shows how to determine if a company has enough staying power.

Going ahead with a project that has insufficient staying power means risking the entire company. Even if the analysis reveals sufficient staying power, management still needs to consider:

The likelihood of the worst case scenario becoming a reality.

The costs of any needed lender assistance.

Management's attitude toward outside interference.

The strategic necessity of the investment.

The potential profitability of the investment.

Since Acme's survival would not be at risk, management might well accept the small-scale option with the intention of embarking on phase two in a year if things go as planned.

A short aside: a company with publicly held bonds usually has less staying power than a company that relies on bank debt and privately placed bonds. If we change the Acme example and assume that the long-term debt was in the form of public bonds, then Acme's bank would have to loan the additional short-term debt that results in the analysis of the small-scale option because arranging principal deferrals on publicly held debt is extremely difficult. Thus Acme's bank would be called on to supply substantial net new money, and it would probably refuse because of the low borrowing base coverage. The conclusion of the analysis would change: the $6.5 million small-scale project is also too risky.

In the late summer of 1981, an oil-field supply company I handled made a large loan request. As part of my due diligence work, I made a telephone survey of executives at some 20 companies involved in various aspects of the energy business to obtain their forecast of drilling activity. The people I called were high-ranking officials at major oil companies, drilling contractors, and large oil-field equipment manufacturers. Virtually every one said that drilling would remain strong for two to five years. I made these calls less than six months before the boom ended.

This incident illustrates how wrong bright and experienced businesspeople can be about their companies' and industries' future. No matter how convinced managers may be of a capital expenditure program's profit potential or strategic necessity, they should take a hard look at the project's downside to make sure the company does not assume an imprudent amount of risk. Staying power analysis is a good way to do this. ▽

Reprint 86502

Success has a lot to do with management's expectations versus results obtained.

Marketing Performance– What Do You Expect?

by Thomas V. Bonoma

A good plot, good friends, and full of expectation; an excellent plot, very good friends.
–Shakespeare,
King Henry IV, Part I

When trying to assess performance, there is no business function top executives worry about more than marketing. Most of them look at the marketers in their companies as something between vacuum-cleaner salespeople and saviors. They fear being sold fancy marketing gizmos they do not want, and they worry that the pledges of marketing salvation will bring real and measurable returns only in a "better world to come."

Yet senior managers still strive to keep the faith. After all, those massive marketing expenditures and fancy programs *may* be doing something that could not be done at less cost or with better results another way. Certainly that's what the marketers and the books say. The question is, how do you know?

Performance is not an absolute thing. The success of a marketing campaign has a lot to do with top management's expectations versus results obtained. Other factors are the effort expended to attain those results and, obviously, elements in the marketplace–like the competition.

In gauging the results, top management may try to overcome its subjective view of the particular campaign and its expectations for it. Being human, executives often stumble at this task. Even when two marketing programs proceed at the same time in the same company, measuring performance can often be a puzzle. Consider, and judge, what happened at the Personal Care Division (PCD) of the Gillette Company a few years ago.

From 1967 to 1982, PCD management had watched Right Guard's po-

sition in the deodorant-antiperspirant market slip from a leading 26% to a fifth-place 8.5% unit share. This was due partly to the chlorofluorocarbon scare in the 1970s and partly to the age of the brand (it had been around since 1960). Still, in 1982, Right Guard was PCD's most important brand, providing 15% of sales but 25% of operating profits. Right Guard, the division determined, needed a massive shot in the arm.

A meticulously documented plan for a radical restage gained acceptance. In a three-year program, PCD would assemble new formulations, packaging, advertising, and pricing to restore the brand's image and reverse its share decline. Expenditures for the restage were formidable; advertising alone for year one of the program would cost $12.7 million.

Results in the first year of the restage, 1983, were mixed. Right Guard missed its unit-share goal by .5%, achieving a 7.6% unit share versus the forecast 8.1%. This was ascribed in part to a larger overall market size than expected; the brand actually beat its forecasts for unit sales, dollar sales, and contribution. Still, research revealed that Right Guard's share of consumers' "last brand purchased" had continued its decade-long decline. For 1984, the division scaled back the restage and adjusted the share forecasts downward.

The pattern of low consumer interest and declining share continued through the mid-1980s. But there were some bright spots: declines in shipments, share, and consumer sales slowed considerably in 1984 and 1985. The direct marketing contribution–the contribution from product sales minus direct marketing expenses–rebounded to its highest level in ten years. Market share, however, sank to 6.5%, which everyone agreed was higher than would have been attained without the program but much lower than management had hoped to reach. By the end

Thomas V. Bonoma is professor of business administration at the Harvard Business School. Currently he teaches marketing in one of the school's executive programs.

of 1986, Right Guard had been designated a "hold" brand, receiving only maintenance spending and positioned to throw off cash to feed other brands. While no one would go on record, the feeling was that the restage had not worked.

PCD's White Rain line went back even further than Right Guard; it was a regional holdover from the 1950s. Consisting of a full "flanker line" of shampoos and other products introduced as late as the 1970s, the brand had seen its line dwindle to a single product, hair spray, and its distribution narrow to the Southern and Central states by the 1980s. But where the hair spray sold well, it sold very well: it held a 10% share in the South.

Noting the popularity of "value" (low-price) brands in the shampoo market, management decided to introduce a value shampoo under the White Rain label to compete with low-end shampoos like Suave and private labels. With the OK of the division president, the brand's managers did virtually no market research. They pushed the program through PCD's traditional planning and control system with a minimum of paperwork, ignoring standard written plans on the grounds that, even if the work was done, the results would be "mostly white space."

PCD launched White Rain shampoo in the South in 1984, using almost no advertising and a quickly devised product formula at 99 cents per unit. The intro was highly positive: the shampoo reached a 2% share in parts of the region.

Encouraged, PCD implemented for 1985 a low-budget national rollout of White Rain and added a conditioner to the shampoo and hair spray. Share figures reached 1.6% for the shampoo and 1.1% for the conditioner, numbers that were not worthy of much consideration in the grander scheme but that blew away the launch forecasts. In addition, the hair spray picked up distribution in several areas where it had been considered dead.

By late 1986, it was apparent that White Rain would exceed its share and shipment forecasts again. Top management was tickled. On the other hand, the brand continued to

lose money. It was not clear when it would become profitable.

The question before the house becomes, which program performed better? You should know that the 100-plus managers and 800 students to whom I've shown the data thought Right Guard performed poorly. The same groups thought White Rain performed well. You should also know that Right Guard has earned more than $90 million for Gillette, $15-20 million of which is acknowledged to be incremental because of the restage. The White Rain launch, like many product introductions, lost money.

How can Gillette's own management, as well as others, maintain that Right Guard failed and White Rain succeeded? Are they right? If so, what factors must be considered to understand the relative performance of the two programs? The answer, of course, lies in management's expectations for the products.

In the case of Right Guard, much was promised, less achieved. The

Market share forecast: 8.1% Actual result: 7.6% Verdict: failure.

restage – a systematic, formal affair – was calculated to halt Right Guard's decline in the market; market share was the critical standard. The brand's managers had submitted a forecast of an 8.1% share in year one of the program and achieved 7.6%. That the brand had exceeded goals for dollar sales, unit sales, and contribution was lost in management's disappointment over share.

White Rain shampoo, on the other hand, promised little. PCD needed to fill a gap in its line of hair care products and had some excess production capacity. Given the brand's loosely conceived, baling-wire national rollout, management had no psychic investment in the product and little hope it would be a hit, even after the pleasantly surprising results of the regional launch. The shampoo's market share forecasts were 1.0% in 1985

and 1.5% in 1986, and for the conditioner, .5% and 1.4% respectively. The shampoo delivered a 1.6% share in 1985 and 3.4% in 1986, while the conditioner produced shares of 1.1% and 2.8% respectively. These results beat top management's expectations and provided great satisfaction. No one expected White Rain to be profitable, so no one cared that it wasn't.

Junior management's role

For the sake of their peace of mind and maybe their jobs, program managers and brand managers have to arrange and conduct their marketing projects to avoid arousing undue optimism on the part of their superiors. Ponder on the error that program management made in the introduction of a liquid dishwashing detergent in the Canadian subsidiary of a packaged goods producer.

The plan promised $3.4 million of operating profit on a full-year launch if top management would authorize some $10 million in first-half expenditures to get things going. But general managers who had no stake in the plan analyzed it and noted several curious things. First, the division was projecting to break even overall for the year, though it had generated a loss in the prior year. Management seemed desperate for a big win. Second, the launch would be the fifth entry in a five-brand category; the four brands in the market were splitting the 30% of consumers who preferred liquid dishwashing detergent. Third, there were no formulation innovations in the proposed product; it was a "me too" item.

Symptoms of overestimation by program management, the "plan yourself out of a jam" approach, can be seen here. Back-loaded rewards were promised for heavy current investments, requiring management to suspend judgment until expenses were fully allocated. A generally unfavorable environment for the entire business produced pressure for "magic plans" that might turn things around. Similar experiences with similar brands produced results far lower than what was being promised. Finally, operating managers with a deep need for salvation were running the business. These signs ar-

One Way to Pay for Performance

Percent of planned operating profit achieved	<95%	95%-100%	100.1%-105%	105.1%-110%	110.1%-120%	>120%
Bonus (percent of total operating profit)	0%	.0001%	.0004%	.0005%	.0006%	.0007%

gued that the program needed to be rethought.

The bane of the marketing manager is the senior manager who constantly thinks your expectations are low and stretches you for more, not on the basis of analysis or even hard thought, but out of habit or hubris. With this type of person, you have only one line of defense: terrifically sound analysis and homework in your planning and the justification of every assumption and scenario you draw. Couple that with a willingness to be fierce about the expectations you have offered, which will be easy if you work hard formulating them and believe in them implicitly. Fight for them. Don't overpromise, don't lie, don't tell the bosses what they want to hear. Fight.

If you're in one of those political situations that can't be fixed with homework and honesty, tell the truth anyway. Better they should hear the news now than at the end of the quarter or year. If nothing does any good, and you're in danger of being accused of causing any low satisfaction that results because you are protesting too much, back off. But put your expectations and your reasons for them on the record. And go ahead and say "I told you so" at the end of the year, but very softly.

There's another scenario, though. You know and I know that you sandbag and maybe "bend" the facts and expectations a little as a matter of corporate living. You are like the sales manager who squirrels away a few orders in a desk folder to ensure making the monthly plan. If you think a 10% share is possible, you'll promise an 8% because how you're going to get paid depends on overachievement, not just achievement. You wouldn't want to miss any bonus, would you? The truth of the matter is that your expectations, at least as you represent them to the bosses, *are* too low, because that's how you know to play it.

You can't have it both ways; either you tell the truth in good times and bad or else you lie all the time. Make up your mind to give senior managers your honest, best shot at what the numbers will be, and then make them understand that you aren't just playing the game but are giving them your best estimate each time out of the box. Over just a little time, this will have a remarkable credibility-building effect for you. People may not like what you say, but they'll come to believe you aren't holding back, playing games, or otherwise "managing" them.

There's nothing senior managers like less than getting "handled" come expectations time. When you do that, you're keeping them from doing their job, which is to get your most accurate estimate so they can gross up over programs and departments in a way that lets them run the business.

The way to keep your own expectations from being too high is to do that homework. Reconsider, then reconsider again. How good is your ex-

ternal intelligence? What do you anticipate competitors will do? Are you positive about costs and about the effort side of the equation? If not, then lower your expectations. If so, try to negotiate a pay-for-performance bonus, then blow the plan out of the water!

Top management's role

We can lay the blame at senior management's doorstep when the expectations for a program are bid up to levels never anticipated or endorsed by those who must execute it. This can leave program management with guaranteed failure—relatively speaking, at least.

When Frito-Lay decided to introduce its Grandma's cookies line nationwide some years ago, the marketing vice president resolved that the results had to at least equal the company's last major launch, that for Tostitos, which produced $130 million in year one. The VP burdened program management with plans for seven plants when three were needed, required a broad cookie line when perhaps concentration on a narrower line would have focused the introduction better, and generally destabilized the program by asking for galactic plans and grand slams when singles would have been welcome. This program was "aspired to

> Don't overpromise to your boss; honesty is still the best policy for program managers.

error" by senior management. (The launch failed, by the way, because it produced "only" $50 million in revenues in under two years, when more than double that was expected.)

The causes of top-down overexpectation include all the ones I cited for bottom-up mistakes but additionally include self-aggrandizement and what might be called "rolling success." Self-aggrandizement marks ego's dominion of realistic thinking in the planning process. Rolling success is particularly pernicious. An instance is the general manager with a string of glorious program triumphs who needs to make each new one a little bigger than the last and sometimes winds up sinking a perfectly good PT boat by welding on it the superstructure of a battleship.

I suggest three steps for senior managers to take when expectations of program managers don't seem to match their own analyses, and politics are not the reason. First, put in place an "I promise" planning system to make explicit the level of confidence you demand before promises are made. That is, if "I believe" a certain market share level is 30% likely, "I think" a level is 50% likely, the "I promise" number is 80% likely, and the "I'm sure" number is 100% likely, then make it clear that you're talking about the "I promise" number, and that's the one you assume will appear in all expectations settings. Put it on the wall. Cole National Corporation has used this procedure with great satisfaction for several years.

Once you have clarified what expectations confidence you're talking about, make sure you offer pay for performance and, additionally, for forecasting accuracy. One subsidiary of Johann Benckiser GmbH, a Ludwigshafen, West Germany marketer of consumer packaged goods, has an incentive plan for program managers that is shown in the chart. Note a key feature apart from its simplicity and the fact that marketers are on profit incentive: the company accelerates the bonus for performance near the point of 100% of plan. Management pays for accuracy too.

Finally, you've got to be very careful not to change the game on the managers. Stories about senior management who've switched from "expecting" share to "expecting" sales or cost reductions in the middle of the period are not only legion, they are also the main reason why your program managers lie to you about what they think they can do.

Reprint 89503

Four Steps to Forecast Total Market Demand

Without a total-demand forecast, you're operating in the dark.

by F. WILLIAM BARNETT

Recent history is filled with stories of companies and sometimes even entire industries that have made grave strategic errors because of inaccurate industrywide demand forecasts. For example:

■ In 1974, U.S. electric utilities made plans to double generating capacity by the mid-1980s based on forecasts of a 7% annual growth in demand. Such forecasts are crucial since companies must begin building new generating plants five to ten years before they are to come on line. But during the 1975-1985 period, load actually grew at only a 2% rate. Despite the postponement or cancellation of many projects, the excess generating capacity has hurt the industry financial situation and led to higher customer rates.

■ The petroleum industry invested $500 billion worldwide in 1980 and 1981 because it expected oil prices to rise 50% by 1985. The estimate was based on forecasts that the market would grow from 52 million barrels of oil a day in 1979 to 60 million barrels in 1985. Instead, demand had fallen to 46 million barrels by 1985. Prices collapsed, creating huge losses in drilling, production, refining, and shipping investments.

■ In 1983 and 1984, 67 new types of business personal computers were introduced to the U.S. market, and most companies were expecting explosive growth. One industry forecasting service projected an installed base of 27 million units by 1988; another predicted 28 million units by 1987. In fact, only 15 million units had been shipped by 1986. By then, many manufacturers had abandoned the PC market or gone out of business altogether.

The inaccurate suppositions did not stem from a lack of forecasting techniques; regression analysis, historical trend smoothing, and others were available to all the players. Instead, they shared a mistaken fundamental assumption: that relationships driving demand in the past would continue unaltered. The companies didn't foresee changes in end-user behavior or understand their market's saturation point. None realized that history can be an unreliable guide as domestic economies become more international, new technologies emerge, and industries evolve.

As a result of changes like these, many managers have come to distrust traditional techniques. Some

even throw up their hands and assume that business planning must proceed without good demand forecasts. I disagree. It is possible to develop valuable insights into future market conditions and demand levels based on a deep understanding of the forces behind total-market demand. These insights can sometimes make the difference between a winning strategy and one that flounders.

A forecast of total-market demand won't guarantee a successful strategy. But without it, decisions on investment, marketing support, and other resource allocations will be based on hidden, unconscious assumptions about industrywide requirements, and they'll often be wrong. By gauging total-market demand explicitly, you have a better chance of controlling your company's destiny. Merely going through the process has merit for a management team. Instead of just coming out with pat answers, numbers, and targets, the team is forced to rethink the competitive environment.

Total-market forecasting is only the first stage in creating a strategy. When you've finished your forecast, you're not done with the planning process by any means.

There are four steps in any total-market forecast:

1. Define the market.
2. Divide total industry demand into its main components.
3. Forecast the drivers of demand in each segment and project how they are likely to change.
4. Conduct sensitivity analyses to understand the most critical assumptions and to gauge risks to the baseline forecast.

Defining the market

At the outset, it's best to be overly inclusive in defining the total market. Define it broadly enough to include *all* potential end users so that you can both identify the appropriate drivers of demand and reduce

Bill Barnett is a principal in the Atlanta office of McKinsey & Company. He is a leader of the firm's Microeconomics Center, and his client work has focused on business unit and corporate strategy.

the risk of surprise product substitutions.

The factors that drive forecasts of total-market size differ markedly from those that determine a particular product's market share or product-category share. For example, total-market demand for office telecommunications products nationally depends in part on the number of people in offices and their needs and habits, while total demand for PBX systems depends on how they compare on price and benefits with substitute products like the local telephone company's central office switching service. Beyond this, demand for a particular PBX is a function of price and benefit comparisons with other PBXs.

In defining the market, an understanding of product substitution is critical. Customers might behave differently if the price or performance of potential substitute products changes. One company studying total demand for industrial paper tubes had to consider closely related uses of metal and plastic tubes to prevent customer switching among tubes from biasing the results.

Understand, too, that a completely new product could displace one that hitherto had comprised the entire market—like the electronic calculator, which eliminated the slide rule. For a while after AT&T's divestiture, the Bell telephone companies continued to forecast volume of long-distance calls by using historical trend lines of their revenues—as if they were still part of a monopoly. Naturally, these forecasts grew more inaccurate with time as end users were presented with new choices. The companies are now broadening their market definitions to take account of heightened competition from other long-distance carriers.

There are several ways you can make sure you include all important substitute products (both current and potential). From interviews with industrial customers you can learn about substitutes they are studying or about product usage patterns that imply future switching opportunities. Moreover, market research can lead to insights about consumer

products. Speaking with experts in the relevant technologies or reviewing technological literature can help you identify potential developments that could threaten your industry.

Finally, careful quantification of the economic value of alternative products to different customers can yield deep insights into potential switching behavior—for example, how oil price movements would affect plastics prices, which in turn would affect plastic products' ability to substitute for metal or paper.

Analyses like these can lead to the construction of industry demand curves—graphs representing the relationship between price and volume. With an appropriate definition, the total-industry demand curves will often be steeper than demand curves for individual products in the industry. Consumers, for example, are far more likely to switch from Maxwell House to Folgers coffee if Maxwell House's prices increase than they are to stop buying coffee if all coffee prices rise.

In some cases, managers can make quick judgments about market definition. In other cases, they'll have to give their market considerable thought and analysis. A total-market forecast may not be critical to business strategy if market definition is very difficult or the products under study have small market shares. Instead, your principal challenge may be to understand product substitution and competitiveness. One company analyzed the potential market for new consumer food cans, and it concluded that growth trends in food product markets were not critical to the strategy question. What was critical was knowing the value positions of the new packages relative to metal cans, glass jars, and composite cans. So the company spent time on that subject.

Dividing demand into component parts

The second step in forecasting is to divide total demand into its main components for separate analysis.

There are two criteria to keep in mind when choosing segments: make each category small and homogeneous enough so that the drivers of

demand will apply consistently across its various elements; make each large enough so that the analysis will be worth the effort. Of course, this is a matter of judgment.

You may find it useful in making this judgment to imagine alternative segmentations (based on end-use customer groups, for example, or type of purchase). Then hypothesize their key drivers of demand (discussed later) and decide how much detail is required to capture the true

> **Americans bought half as many computers as the industry had predicted.**

situation. As the assessment continues, managers can return to this stage and reexamine whether the initial decisions still stand up.

Managers may wish to use a "tree" diagram like the accompanying one constructed by a management team in 1985 to study demand for paper. In this disguised example, industry data permitted the division of demand into 12 end-use categories. Some categories, like business forms and reprographic paper, were big contributors to total consumption; others, such as labels, were not. One (other converting) was fairly large but too diverse for deep analysis. The team focused on the four segments that accounted for 80% of 1985 demand. It then developed secondary branches of the tree to further dissect these categories and to determine their drivers of demand. It analyzed the remaining segments less completely (that is, via a regression against broad macroeconomic trends).

Other companies have used similar methods to segment total demand. One company divided demand for maritime satellite terminals by type of ship (e.g., seismic ships, bulk/cargo/container ships). Another divided demand for long-distance telephone service into business and residential customers

Components of Uncoated White Paper Making Up Total Demand (thousands of tons)

	End-Use Category	Percent of Total 1985 Demand
Total Demand	Business Forms	25%
	Commercial Printing	25
	Reprographics	20
	Envelopes	10
	Other Converting	5
	Stationery and Tablet	5
	Books	5
	Directories	1 or less
	Catalogs	
	Magazines	
	Inserts	
	Labels	

Reviewed in Depth

and then subdivided it by usage level. And a third segmented consumer appliances into three purchase types—appliances used in new home construction, replacement appliance sales in existing homes, and appliance penetration in existing homes.

In thinking about market divisions, managers need to decide whether to use existing data on segment sizes or to commission research to get an independent estimate. Reliable public information on historical demand levels by segment is available for many big U.S. industries (like steel, automobiles, and natural gas) from industry associations, the federal government, off-the-shelf studies by industry experts, or ongoing market data services. For some foreign markets and less well-researched industries in the United States, like the labels industry, you may have to get independent estimates. Even with good data sources, however, the readily available information may not be divided into the best categories to support an insightful analysis. In these cases, managers must decide whether to develop their forecasts based on the available historical data or

to undertake their own market research programs, which can be time-consuming and expensive.

Note that while such segmentation is sufficient for forecasting total demand, it may not create categories useful for developing a marketing strategy. A single product may be driven by entirely different factors. One study of industrial components found that consumer industry categories provided a good basis for projecting total-market demand but gave only limited help in formulating a strategy based on customer preferences: distinguishing those who buy on price from those who buy on service, product quality, or other benefits. Such buying-factor categories generally do not correlate with the customer industry categories used for forecasting. A strong sales force, however, can identify customer preferences and develop appropriate account tactics for each one.

Forecasting the drivers of demand

The third step is to understand and forecast the drivers of demand in each category. Here you can make

good use of regressions and other statistical techniques to find some causes for changes in historical demand. But this is only a start. The tougher challenge is to look beyond the data on which regressions can easily be based to other factors where data are much harder to find. Then you need to develop a point of view on how those other factors may themselves change in the future.

An end-use analysis from the commodity paper example, reprographic paper, is shown in the accompanying chart. The management team, using available data, divided reprographic paper into two categories: plain-paper copier paper and nonimpact page printer paper. Without this important differentiation, the drivers of demand would have been masked, making it hard to forecast effectively.

In most cases, managers can safely assume that demand is affected both by macroeconomic variables and by industry-specific developments. In looking at plain-paper copier paper, the team used simple and multiple regression analyses to test relationships with macroeconomic factors like white-collar workers, population, and economic performance. Most of the factors had a significant effect on demand. Intuitively, it also made sense to the team that the level of business activity would relate to paper consumption levels. (Economists sometimes refer to growth in demand due to factors like these as an "outward shift" in the demand curve—toward a greater quantity demanded at a given price.)

Demand growth for copy paper, however, had exceeded the real rate of economic growth and the challenge was to find what other factors had been causing this. The team hypothesized that declining copy costs had caused this increased usage. The relationship was proved by estimating the substantial cost reductions that had occurred, combining those with numbers of tons produced over time, and then fashioning an indicative demand curve for copy paper. (See the chart "Understanding Copy Paper Demand Drivers.") The clear relationship between cost and volume meant that cost

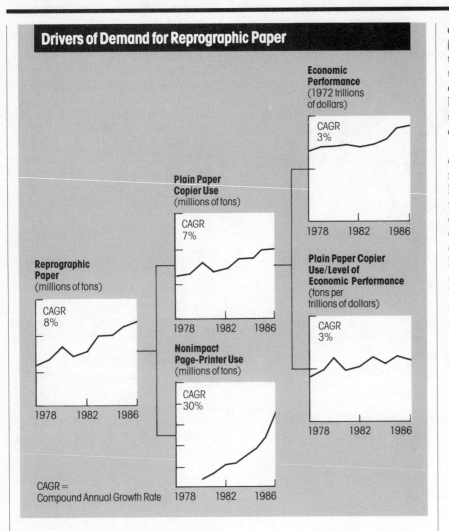

Drivers of Demand for Reprographic Paper

Economic Performance
(1972 trillions of dollars)
CAGR 3%
1978   1982   1986

Plain Paper Copier Use
(millions of tons)
CAGR 7%
1978   1982   1986

Reprographic Paper
(millions of tons)
CAGR 8%
1978   1982   1986

Plain Paper Copier Use/Level of Economic Performance
(tons per trillions of dollars)
CAGR 3%
1978   1982   1986

Nonimpact Page-Printer Use
(millions of tons)
CAGR 30%
1978   1982   1986

CAGR = Compound Annual Growth Rate

reductions had been an important cause of past demand growth. (Economists sometimes describe this as a downward-shifting supply curve leading to movement down the demand curve.)

Further major declines in cost per copy seemed unlikely because paper costs were expected to remain flat, and the data indicated little increase in price elasticity, even if cost per copy fell further. So the team concluded that usage growth (per level of economic performance) was likely to continue the flattening trend begun in 1983: growth in copy paper consumption would be largely a function of economic growth, not cost declines as in the past. The team then reviewed several econometric services forecasts to develop a base case economic forecast.

Similar studies have been performed in other industries. A simple one was the industrial components analysis mentioned before, a case where the total forecast was used as background but was not critical to the company's strategy decision. Here the team divided demand into its consuming industries and then asked experts in each industry for production forecasts. Total demand for components was projected on the assumption that it would move parallel to a weight-averaged forecast of these customer industries. Actual demand three years later was 2% above the team's prediction, probably because the industry experts underestimated the impact of the economic recovery of 1984 and 1985.

In another example, a team forecasting demand for maritime satellite terminals extrapolated past penetration curves for each of five categories of ships. These curves were then adjusted for major

changes in the shipping industry (e.g., adding the depressing effect of the growing oil glut, taking out of these historical trends the unnatural demand growth that had been caused by the Falklands war). The actual figure three years later was within 1% of the forecast.

Knowing the drivers of demand is crucial to the success of any total-market demand forecast. In 1974, as I mentioned earlier, most electric utilities used an incomplete total-demand forecast to predict robust demand growth. In the early 1980s, one company's management team, however, decided to study potential changes in end-user demand as well. The team divided electricity demand into the three traditional categories: residential, commercial, and industrial. It then profiled differences in residential demand because of more efficiency in home appliances and changes in home size and the ratio of multi-unit to single-family dwellings. Industrial demand was analyzed by evaluating the future of several key consuming industries, paying special attention to changes in their total production and electricity use. This end-use approach sharply reduced the utility's initial forecasts and led to cancellation of two $700 million generating plants then in the planning stage.

In 1983, forecasters in the U.S. personal computer industry were saying that demand would continue to rise at a rapid rate because there were 50 million white-collar workers and only 8 million installed PCs. One company, however, did a more detailed demand forecast that showed that growth would soon flatten out. It found that more than two-thirds of white-collar workers either did not require PCs in their jobs—actors and elevator operators, for instance—or were supported mostly by inexpensive terminals linked to large computers, as in the case of many clerical workers. The potential market was not big enough to support the growth rate. Indeed, the market began to flatten the next year.

Forecasting total demand became crucial for another company that was thinking about acquiring a maker of video games. Many thought

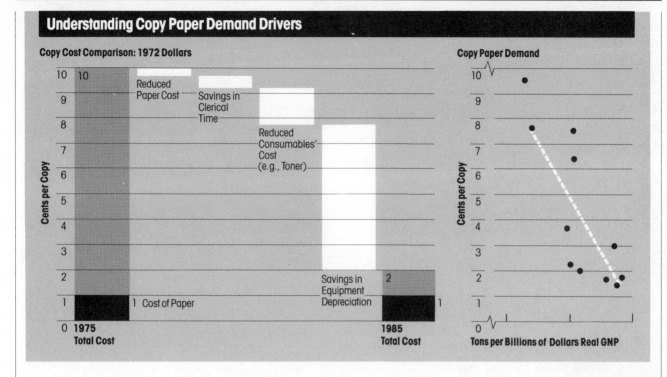

Understanding Copy Paper Demand Drivers

Copy Cost Comparison: 1972 Dollars

(Cents per Copy)

- 1975 Total Cost: 10
- Reduced Paper Cost
- Savings in Clerical Time
- Reduced Consumables' Cost (e.g., Toner)
- Savings in Equipment Depreciation
- Cost of Paper: 1
- 1985 Total Cost: 2 / 1

Copy Paper Demand

(Cents per Copy)

Tons per Billions of Dollars Real GNP

---

that low overall market penetration (10% of U.S. households) signified a lot of room for growth before the market became saturated, when about 50% of the households would have games. Using available data, however, the management team created categories based on family income and children's ages. The analysis made clear that the main target market, upper-income families with children, was already well penetrated. Families with incomes exceeding $50,000 and children between the ages of 6 and 15 already were 75% penetrated. This finding convinced management that demand would fall and that the proposed acquisition did not make sense. The dramatic decline in video game sales shortly thereafter confirmed the wisdom of this judgment.

Conducting sensitivity analyses

Managers who rely on single-point demand forecasts run dangerous risks. Some of the macroeconomic variables behind the forecasts could be wrong. Despite the best analysis, moreover, the assumptions behind the other demand drivers could also be wrong, especially if disconti-

nuities loom on the horizon. Imaginative marketers who ask questions like "What things could cause this forecast to change dramatically?" produce the best estimates. They are more likely to identify potential risks and discontinuities – developments in competing technologies, in customer industry competitiveness, in supplier cost structures – than those who do not. So once a baseline forecast is complete, the challenge is to determine how far it could be off target.

At one level, such a sensitivity analysis can be done by simply varying assumptions and quantifying their impact on demand. But a more targeted approach usually provides better insight.

Begin such an analysis by thinking through and quantifying the areas of greatest strategic risk. One company's strategy decision may be affected only if demand is well below the baseline forecast; in another case, big risks may result from small forecasting errors.

Next, gauge the likelihood of such a development. In the white paper example, the baseline forecast called for continued market growth, though below historical levels. In any particular year, demand could

fluctuate with the economy, but the critical question was whether demand would at some point begin a long decline. If so, the companion supply-curve analysis indicated that prices would probably fall dramatically.

The team created two scenarios of a gradual decline, one based largely on changes in the economy and the other on changes in assumed end-use trends. These scenarios showed what would make demand fall (e.g., different rates of decline in copier prices) and thereby provided a basis for evaluating the likelihood of a downturn.

Determining an appropriate effort

The forecasting framework outlined above can work for both comprehensive and simple assessments, but there are different ways to carry out these analyses. A big challenge in demand forecasting (just as with other types of market analysis) is to gauge the appropriate effort for the project's purpose. It's useful to ask: "How much do I need to know to make the decision at hand?"

Managers can invest a lot of time in such analyses – the paper example took about 8 man-weeks and the large-scale electricity forecast about 14 man-weeks. Some companies have forecasting departments who work year-round on these subjects. The more thorough, though time-consuming, approach generates greater confidence, and the effort will be appropriate where the demand projection can significantly influence corporate strategy (whether to make a several hundred million dollar capital investment, for example), or where there is great uncertainty about total demand.

Often, however, the issues are not complicated, time is limited, or the total demand forecast is not important enough to merit that commitment (for example, the company is looking to add a couple of points to its small market share). In such cases, managers should proceed quickly and inexpensively. They can, for example, rely on experts' judgment or unsophisticated regressions to forecast drivers of demand. Even the limited approaches can yield insights. Furthermore, beginning the demand analysis process can help managers determine whether important demand issues exist that should be analyzed in greater depth.

Total-demand forecasting can be important to strategy decisions. Developing independent forecasts through the four-step framework I've outlined will not only lead to better recommendations but also help build conviction and consensus for action by creating understanding of the drivers of demand and the risks in forecasts.

Even when the work is sound, though, uncertainties will remain: discontinuities will still be difficult to predict, especially if they are rooted in momentous political, macroeconomic, or technological changes. But managers who push their thinking through the steps in this framework will have a better chance of finding these discontinuities than those who do not. And those who base their business strategies on a solid knowledge of demand will stand a much greater chance of making wise investments and competing effectively.

Reprint 88401

Decision making: going forward in reverse

Hillel J. Einhorn and Robin M. Hogarth

Busy managers analyze many situations and make hundreds of decisions every day. Why, for example, are sales up in one city but down in another? Would an investment in new equipment mean higher productivity or greater confusion? Is now a good time to look for a joint venture partner, or is it better to wait? Rarely, however, do we stop to think about how we think. Each decision is the outcome of a complex process that usually involves two different kinds of thinking: looking backward to understand the past and looking forward to predict the future.

Thinking backward is largely intuitive and suggestive; it tends to be diagnostic and requires judgment. It involves looking for patterns, making links between seemingly unconnected events, testing possible chains of causation to explain an event, and finding a metaphor or a theory to help in looking forward.

Thinking forward is different. Instead of intuition, it depends on a kind of mathematical formulation: the decision maker must assemble and weigh a number of variables and then make a prediction. Using a strategy or a rule, assessing the accuracy of each factor, and combining all the pieces of information, the decision maker arrives at a single, integrated forecast.

Although managers use both types of thinking all the time, they are often unaware of the differences. Moreover, this lack of awareness makes decision makers stumble into mental traps that yield bad decisions. By understanding thinking backward and forward, we can recognize these traps and improve our decisions.

Thinking backward

To understand how thinking backward works, think back to the days of the cave dwellers and consider the following exercise in assessing cause and effect. Imagine that you belong to a tribe that is sophisticated in methodology but primitive in science. Your tribe has very little knowledge of biology, physics, or chemistry but a very big problem—an alarming decrease in the birthrate. The problem is so severe that the tribe's statistician estimates that unless you can reverse the trend soon, the tribe will become extinct.

To respond to the crisis, the chief urgently launches a project to determine the cause of birth. As a member of the project team assigned the task of linking cause and effect, you have been assured that you will be allowed any and all forms of experimentation, including the use of your fellow tribespersons, to resolve this critical issue.

> *"Why a simple decision isn't."*

The first question, of course, is what to consider a relevant causal factor. In searching for a link between cause and effect, most people usually look first to some unusual or remarkable event or condition that preceded the effect. In this case, you might ask yourself if something unusual happened before the decline in births. You might look for evidence of the cause of the problem that is similar in some way to the outcome—similar in some physical or metaphorical way. Then you could assess the likelihood that the evidence explains the problem.

You might notice that the children in your tribe are similar in appearance to men and women who live together. This similarity could lead you to a leap of intuition backward: sexual intercourse causes pregnancy. You and the members of your study team

Hillel J. Einhorn is the Wallace W. Booth Professor of Behavioral Science at the University of Chicago Graduate School of Business and the founder and former director of its Center for Decision Research. Robin M. Hogarth is professor of behavioral science at the University of Chicago Graduate School of Business and director of the Center for Decision Research.

would probably acknowledge, however, that this theory is unproven, indeed unsupported. First, there's a big gap between cause and effect—nine months, to be exact. Second, you have no knowledge of the sequence of biological processes that link intercourse and pregnancy, no knowledge of the causal chain. Third, the cause and the effect are very different in scale and duration. And fourth, many other factors that may correlate with intercourse are difficult to rule out—for example, sitting under a palm tree and holding hands in full moonlight (an explanation once advanced in a letter to "Dear Abby").

There is only one way to settle the issue and save the tribe from extinction: conduct an experiment. From a sample of 200 couples, you assign 100 to test intercourse and 100 to test nonintercourse. After some time, you get the following results: of the 100 couples assigned to test intercourse, 20 became pregnant and 80 did not; of the 100 assigned to test nonintercourse, 5 became pregnant and 95 did not. (These five pregnancies represent a fairly typical measurement error in such data and can be explained by faulty memory, lying, and human frailty.)

With the results in hand, you calculate the correlation between intercourse and pregnancy and find that it is .34. Since this correlation is only modest, you conclude that intercourse is not a major factor in causing pregnancy. You discard your unsupported theory and press on for another solution. Could there be something to that palm tree theory, after all?

Three steps back

This example illustrates the three interrelated phases of thinking backward: finding relevant variables, linking them in a causal chain, and assessing the plausibility of the chain.

The search for an explanation often begins when we notice that something is different, unusual, or wrong. Usually, it takes an unexpected event to pique our curiosity—we are rarely interested in finding out why we feel "average" or why traffic is flowing "normally." In the case of our cave dwellers, the declining birthrate is both unusual and threatening and therefore stimulates remedial action.

The next step is to look for some relevant causal factor, to focus on some abnormal event that resembles the unusual outcome in a number of ways: it may be similar in scale, in how long it lasts, or in when it happens. Most people harbor the notion that similar causes have similar effects. For example, according to "the doctrine of signatures," adopted in early Western medicine, diseases are caused or cured by substances that physically resemble them. Thus, a cure for jaundice would be yellow, and so on. As strange as that

may seem, it is also difficult to imagine how we could search for variables without looking for some kind of similarity between cause and effect.

The search for similarity often involves analogy and metaphor. In trying to understand how the brain works, for instance, we can imagine it as a computer, a muscle, or a sponge. Each metaphor suggests a different way of picturing the brain's processes. A computer suggests information input, storage, retrieval, and computation. A muscle suggests building power through use and loss of strength because of atrophy or the strain of overuse. A sponge suggests the passive absorption of information. The metaphor we choose in describing the brain—or in understanding any link between cause and effect—is critical since it directs attention to one way of thinking.

The search for causally relevant variables goes hand in hand with the consideration of indicators, or "cues to causality," that suggest some probable link between cause and effect. There are four categories of cues: temporal order (causes happen before effects), proximity (causes are generally close to effects in time and space), correlation (causes tend to vary along with effects), and similarity (causes may resemble effects through analogy and metaphor or in length and strength).

These cues to causality do not necessarily prove a link between cause and effect. They do, however, indicate likely directions in which to seek relevant variables and limit the number of scenarios or chains that can be constructed between possible causes and their supposed effects.

How likely is it, for example, that sunspots cause price changes on the stock market? Before you dismiss this as an absurd hypothesis, consider that the eminent nineteenth-century economist William Stanley Jevons believed in such a link. To make this link, you have to construct a causal chain that meets various constraints. For the sake of discussion, let's assume that at a certain time some sunspots did occur before price changes (the temporal order is correct); that when the sun had sunspot activity, there were many price changes (the correlation is positive); and that these price changes occurred six months after sunspot activity (the proximity in time is not very close). The task is to bridge the time lag and distance gap between sunspots and price changes. If you cannot do so, you cannot prove a causal relationship.

Now consider the following chain: sunspots affect weather conditions, which affect agricultural production, which affects economic conditions, which affect profits, which affect stock prices. The cues to causality constrain the possible chains that you can imagine. This constraint is especially important in evaluating the cue of temporal order: for one event to cause another, it must precede it. But the cues of proximity in time and space, of congruity, and of the length and strength of cause and effect also constrain the linkage. The way to bridge the spatial and temporal gaps between the sunspots and the stock market changes is to look for a change in the weather.

Imagine, however, that price changes occur immediately after sunspot activity rather than six months later. The closeness in time between the two events eliminates the link between weather and these economic conditions, which requires a time delay. To link sunspots and price changes, you would have to come up with another scenario that meets the test of proximity in time.

Another test that the cues to causality suggest is incongruity—that is, small causes that yield big effects or big causes that produce small effects. To account for these apparent discrepancies, the causal chain must involve some kind of amplification in the first case and some sort of reduction in the second. When Louis Pasteur advanced the germ theory of disease in the 1800s, for example, it must have seemed incredible to his contemporaries, solely because of the test of incongruity. How could tiny, invisible creatures cause disease, plague, and death? In the absence of scientific information, people saw no causal chain that could amplify such minute causes to such enormous effects.

Better thinking backward

Several approaches can improve the way we make thinking backward work in decision making:

1   **Use several metaphors.** Because backward thinking is both intuitive and swift, most people can generate a single metaphor quickly and expand it into an extensive causal chain. But all metaphors are imperfect. When you use them, it is important to remember the old adage that the map is not the territory.

Using several metaphors can be a guard against prematurely adopting a single model. Instead of focusing on one metaphor, experiment with several. Consider, for example, how you might think about complex organizations such as graduate schools of business. Each metaphor illuminates a different dimension of the subject. You could think of business schools as finishing schools, where students mature appropriately before entering corporate life; as military academies, where students prepare for economic warfare; as monasteries, where students receive indoctrination in economic theology; as diploma mills, where students receive certification; or as job shops, where students are tooled to perform specific tasks.

Each metaphor illustrates a different factor, an alternative way of thinking. No metaphor by

itself is adequate; considering them all provides a more complete picture.

2   **Do not rely on one cue alone.** Inferring causality from just one cue often leads to serious error. Because they relied on a single measure, the cave dwellers diverted their attention from the real cause of pregnancy. Correlation does not always imply causation, nor does causation always imply correlation.

3   **Sometimes go against the cues.** A great benefit of the cues is that they give structure to our perceptions and help us interpret ambiguous information. But there is a trade-off between this structure and novelty and originality. The cues help by directing attention to what is obvious and reducing alternative interpretations. But the hallmark of insights is that they surprise us. One way to promote creative thinking, then, is to go against the cues. When searching for an explanation for a complex outcome, sometimes look for a simple or a dissimilar cause rather than a complex or a similar one.

4   **Assess causal chains.** The way to test potential causes and effects is through a causal chain, but the strength of each chain varies. The chain connecting sunspots and stock prices, for instance, is weak because there are so many links and each is uncertain. In fact, most causal chains are only as strong as their weakest links, and long chains are generally weaker than short ones. But research indicates that people do not always grasp these facts. Many people regard complex scenarios with detailed outcomes as much more coherent—and thus much more likely—than simple ones. It is important to evaluate chains according to the number and strength of their links.

5   **Generate and test alternative explanations.** Most people have a natural aptitude for thinking diagnostically. But one of its drawbacks is that it can lead to superstitions that hold sway for long periods. The history of medicine is full of them. For many years, doctors used bloodletting, for instance, as a popular and presumably scientifically sound cure. Could our most cherished theories about economics and business in time become as obsolete as bloodletting?

Experiments can guard against superstition. To assess the effectiveness of advertising, for example, you could conduct experiments by stopping advertising completely. If it is not feasible to go to such extremes, you could use partial tests, which can give you much useful information: you could stop advertising only in certain areas or for certain periods.

If you can't do such an experiment, you can nevertheless imagine situations in which the effect occurs without the suspected cause. In imaginary scenarios, you can judge causal links. The question under consideration may be whether a particular advertising campaign has caused an increase in sales. By trying to answer the question, Would sales have risen without the advertising campaign? you can get an esti-

"Well, it so happens I've diversified. I'm now the hobgoblins of big and medium as well as little minds."

mate of the proper link between sales and advertising. A worthwhile experiment would include a second question: Will sales go up if we advertise? By posing these questions in a systematic way, you can get information almost as useful and powerful as what you get from actually trying something out.

Thinking forward

Whether we like to acknowledge it or not, most of the time we do a poor job of thinking forward with any accuracy. Evidence gathered in such diverse fields as marriage counseling, bank lending, economic forecasting, and psychological counseling indicates that most human predictions are less accurate than even the simplest statistical models.

Most people have more faith in human judgment, however, than in statistical models. The disadvantages of statistical models compared with human judgment seem obvious. Or so the argument goes. But is this right? Let's consider the evidence.

Models make errors. The use of a formal model implies trade-offs; a model will make errors since it is an abstraction that cannot possibly capture the full richness of the relations between variables. Human judgment, on the other hand, can sometimes capitalize on idiosyncratic features that are difficult or impossible to model.

Human judgment can also result in errors, but models are perfectly consistent; they never get bored, tired, or distracted, as people do. Models are never inconsistent or random—in fact, they may be consistent to a fault. The important question, then, is which method leads to less overall error.

Or to put the question another way, if we accept the inevitability of some error from using a formal model, will we end up with less overall error by using the model rather than human judgment? According to the results of psychological experiments on probability learning, the answer is yes.

In these studies, subjects are asked to predict which of two lights— one red, one green—will go on. If they guess right, the subjects get a cash reward. If they guess wrong, they get no reward. A random process governs which light goes on, but by arrangement, the red light goes on 60% of the time and the green light, 40%. Subjects are not told about the percentages but have the opportunity to learn about them by participating in the experiment.

The result of this kind of experiment is something called probability matching: subjects learn to respond to cues in the same proportion as they occur. In this case, subjects predict red about 60% of the time and green, 40%. And yet they do not come up with the best predictive strategy that will gain the greatest cash reward, because they are unwilling to accept error.

By predicting red 60% of the time and green 40%, subjects can expect to be right a total of 52% of the time: they will be right on the red light 36% of the time and right on the green light 16% of the time.

But what would happen if subjects were willing to predict red, the more likely color, every time? Such a strategy accepts error; it also leads to 60% correct prediction—8% higher than a strategy that seeks the right answer on every guess.

The subjects would make more money if they accepted error and consistently used a simple mathematical model. Most subjects try to predict perfectly, though, and futilely attempt to discern some nonexistent rule or pattern that determines which light will go on. Any similarity between this example and playing the stock market is purely coincidental.

Models are static. This criticism is simply not true. Models can and should be updated with new information as it becomes available. Models are now being developed that learn from the outcomes of predicted events. This work, while still in its early stages, suggests models can learn from experience.

As far as human judgment is concerned, it is simply not clear that people do learn from feedback in making predictions. Part of the difficulty in learning occurs when people make predictive judgments to take action. The outcomes provide only ambiguous feedback on the quality of the predictions.

For example, imagine a case in which the president of the United States takes strong measures to counteract a predicted economic slowdown. Now consider the difficulties of learning from the various possible outcomes. Imagine having no recession as an outcome. This could result either from an incorrect prediction and an ineffective action or from an accurate prediction and a highly effective action. Now imagine a recession as an outcome. This could result either from an accurate prediction and an ineffective action or from an inaccurate prediction and a boomerang action that causes the very malady it is intended to prevent. The problem is this: to learn about our predictive ability requires separating the quality of predictions from the effects of actions based on those predictions.

Models are not worth their cost. In general, it is impossible to evaluate the argument that any marginal increase in accuracy from using models does not outweigh the extra cost of building them. If a model is used to make enough predictions, however, even small increases in accuracy can produce large benefits.

For example, in the late 1970s, AT&T conducted a study to determine the characteristics of good and bad credit risks.[1] Management incorporated the results in a set of decision rules that it used to determine which new customers should be required to provide deposits. In developing these rules, AT&T went through a time when it granted credit to customers it would have previously classified as both good risks and bad risks. As a result, the rules were validated across the whole range of customer characteristics. By implementing the decision rules, management realized an estimated annual reduction of $137 million in bad debts. While no figures are available on the cost of creating and maintaining the model, it is difficult to believe that the savings did not warrant the expense.

While many phenomena we try to predict are complex, the rules for reasoning forward need not match this complexity. Many successful applications have involved simple combinations of just a few variables. Sometimes the rules develop from modeling an expert's past judgments, sometimes simply by averaging past decisions, and sometimes just by aggregating a few relevant variables.

Backward & forward

Our everyday experience is filled with examples of thinking backward and thinking forward. We are constantly using both modes of reasoning, separately and together, and we are constantly confounded in our efforts.

While explicit rules or models are the best tools to use for reasoning forward, intuition or notions of cause can often exert a powerful influence on the predictions we make. When people take actions in situations where random processes produce the outcomes, they are sometimes subject to delusions of control. For instance, people tend to believe that lottery tickets they personally select have a greater chance of winning than those selected for them by a lottery administrator.

By the same token, in complex situations, we may rely too heavily on planning and forecasting and underestimate the importance of random factors in the environment. That reliance can also lead to delusions of control. The best posture is to remain skeptical toward all undocumented claims of predictive accuracy, whether they are derived from experts, models, or both. Remember the seersucker theory of prediction: for every seer, there is a sucker.[2]

An important paper on how to improve predictive ability once expressed the task of thinking forward in this way: "The whole trick is to decide what variables to look at and then know how to add."[3] But "the trick" is a difficult one that requires complex thinking backward. Indeed, computer scientists who are working to build programs that simulate the understanding process by means of artificial intelligence have had great difficulty in modeling this process. A recent example concerns a program they wrote to simulate the comprehension of newspaper headlines. They provided the program with background knowledge and a set of rules to rewrite the headlines. One such headline was: "World shaken. Pope shot." The computer interpreted this as: "Earthquake in Italy. One dead."

Although the psychological study of judgment and decision making has concentrated on separating thinking backward from thinking forward by clarifying the distinction, the two modes of reasoning are interdependent. Like the god Janus in Roman mythology, whose head has two faces, one facing forward, the other backward, our thinking goes in both directions whenever we put our minds to work on making a decision. ⊟

1 J.L. Showers and L.M. Chakrin, "Reducing Uncollectible Revenue from Residential Telephone Customers," *Interfaces*, December 1981, p. 21.

2 J.Scott Armstrong, *Long-Range Forecasting* (New York: Wiley, 1978).

3 Robyn M. Dawes and Bernard Corrigan, "Linear Models in Decision Making," *Psychological Bulletin*, February 1974, p. 95.

Reprint 87107

Keeping Informed

*Peter L. Bernstein and
Theodore H. Silbert*

Are economic forecasters worth listening to?

Yes, on a consensus basis; heeding them is preferable to planning as if tomorrow will be much like today

*Are forecasters ever wrong?
At one time or another, every professional forecaster is wrong. Taken as a group, however, forecasters have a good record, this article asserts. Reliance on a consensus outlook can at least keep you aware of signs that current trends are changing. These kinds of signals can help the corporate executive avoid victimization by the ups and downs of business cycles—such as being fully stocked and expecting more materials to come into inventory, just as the economy takes a nose dive.*

Mr. Bernstein heads his own economic and financial consulting firm in New York City. He is also editor of the Journal of Portfolio Management. *Mr. Silbert is founder and board chairman of Sterling National Bank & Trust Company, New York City. Three years ago he established an annual award for accuracy in economic forecasting, which is administered at the Graduate School of Business, Columbia University. The first winner was James L. Pate, the vice president and treasurer of Pennzoil Company, the second was Charles B. Reeder, the chief economist of DuPont, and the third, in 1983, was Peter Bernstein.*

**"I hope you'll keep in mind that economic forecasting is far from a perfect science. If recent history's any guide, the experts have some explaining to do about what they told us had to happen but never did."
Ronald Reagan
January 21, 1984**

**"Since the destruction of the Second Temple, prophecy has become the lot of fools."
Hebrew expression**

From Herbert Hoover's happy prediction that prosperity was just around the corner to Ronald Reagan's steadfast promise in October 1980 that the fiscal 1984 budget would show a $30 billion surplus, economic forecasts have been wrong. Often, indeed, they have been in wild disagreement with one another. In December 1981, for example, when the winds of recession were beginning to blow strongly, the 44 leading economic forecasting services covered by Robert Eggert's Blue Chip Economic Indicators, a monthly publication, showed predictions for real GNP growth in 1982 that ranged all the way from +4.0% over 1981 by the most optimistic forecaster to

−1.7% change by the gloomiest. Their expectations for pretax profits ranged all the way from −19.9% to +19.0%!

This is all very amusing, but it suggests some serious questions. Given the frailties of the process, can forecasts have any value for business executives who have to make decisions about how much inventory to carry, how aggressively to price their products, how vigorously to resist wage demands, and when and how to finance expansion? If not, whom can they believe?

And even if they can answer these difficult questions, why should they bother with economic outlooks in the first place? Is there a cost for ignoring them and listening only to the signals from their own companies and their own industries?

We argue that economic forecasts deserve to be taken seriously, not necessarily because they promise to be accurate but because they are so much more useful than having no forecasts at all. We do not say that managers should listen to all forecasts or to all forecasters; that is the sure road to total confusion. Rather, we say that forecasts properly used and understood will lead to better business decisions than forecasts ignored or naively used.

Better than nothing?

A respectable body of thought argues that expectations are so rapidly embodied in decisions that no one can make forecasts better than those implicit in the marketplace itself. This viewpoint has enjoyed most prominence in markets where pricing is based on expectations, such as the stock and bond markets and the markets for commodity futures.

Some observers argue also that even the pricing of nonfinancial goods and services, including labor, reflects anticipation of conditions to

1 "The Track Record of Macroeconomic Forecasts," *New England Economic Review,* November-December 1983, p. 5.

2 "The Accuracy of Individual and Group Forecasts from Business Outlook Surveys," National Bureau of Economic Research, Working Paper 1053, December 1982, pp. 9-10.

such an extent that forecasting the next change – in either direction or of any magnitude – is likely to be hazardous. The best forecast may simply be that tomorrow will look like today or like today's trends extrapolated to tomorrow.

Note that the proponents of this position do not argue that these implicit forecasts in the marketplace will be correct. They know better. They do say, however, that these forecasts will be less wrong than the predictions of individuals who think they know more than the millions of forecasts already imbedded in the market by the real-time decisions of participants in it.

While the financial markets offer enough evidence to justify taking this view seriously, it is much more controversial when we look at it in terms of the economy. Unlike the movement of actively traded financial assets (which may indeed have the features of a random walk), the swings in real GNP, inflation, unemployment, industrial production, and earnings are part of a process, a process in which one stage leads inexorably to the next and in which decisions once made are difficult to reverse. Only the timing of the process is hard to predict; its fundamental character is by no means obscure.

Hence the expectation that tomorrow's figures will be the same as today's, or an extrapolation of today's trends, is certain to be wrong. In fact, it is likely to be more wrong than a careful prediction based on some understanding of the process that leads the business cycle to evolve from today to tomorrow.

Suppose it is 1972 and you are sitting and contemplating the outlook for 1973 or 1974. Since 1952 the annual change in real GNP has averaged 3.4%, with a standard deviation of 2.3 percentage points. Your first problem is the 65% probability that real growth in 1973 could be between 1.7% and 5.7% – a spread so wide relative to the mean growth rate that your only rational expectation would be that *anything* could happen in 1973 and 1974.

As we know, that is precisely what did occur: real GNP in 1973 was 0.6% below 1972, while in 1974 it fell 1.2% below 1973. These changes came even outside the band of one standard deviation around the mean. If you had been playing around with an inflation

forecast on the same basis, your estimates would have been catastrophically off base.

We can find a more elegant demonstration of the weakness of extrapolative techniques in an analysis of forecast accuracy by Stephen McNees and John Ries, economists at the Federal Reserve Bank of Boston.[1] McNees and Ries studied the performance of a group of leading forecasting organizations as measured by their quarterly forecasts of principal economic variables from the first quarter of 1971 through the second quarter of 1983.

The researchers also provided a benchmark "forecast" – an unconditional autoregressive moving-average time series based only on the past historical values of the predicted variables. This so-called ARIMA technique is the most sophisticated procedure available for extrapolating past trends into the future. Where the forecasted series has the essential elements of a random walk, the ARIMA forecast will outperform conventional extrapolation forecasts with a high degree of probability.

McNees and Ries used this benchmark projection for real GNP and for nominal GNP (which equals real GNP times the inflation rate) for forecasts made early each quarter for the current quarter and each of the three following quarters. Overall, the benchmark ranked lowest among the six other forecasts in the test. It was not the worst estimate in every single quarter, but it was always close to the worst. Its average error of 2.80 percentage points for real GNP contrasts with 2.68 for the worst conventional forecast and 2.39 for the group as a whole. Its error for nominal GNP averaged 3.83 points, as against 3.78 points for the worst conventional forecast and 3.34 points for the group.

In short, when it comes to making judgments about the outlook for the real economy, you are better off listening to professional forecasters than acting on the assumption that anything can happen or that tomorrow will simply reflect trends in effect today.

But which forecaster?

The yawning gap between the most optimistic and the most pessimistic participants in the Blue Chip survey for 1982 was not an extreme or even an atypical case. Forecasters often disagree, so that some of them are certain to be wrong. If some of them were wrong all the time, chances are that the poor folks would not continue in business. So we have no prima facie method for knowing which ones will be on target, or even close to the target, in any given situation.

The track records of particular forecasters are even more confusing. McNees and Ries showed that the best forecaster in any one year had little assurance of coming out on top in the following year. Furthermore, some were better than others at predicting, for instance, the course of prices or production or government spending. On some occasions, however, the superior price forecasters were better on the consumer price index than on the GNP deflator, and sometimes the results were the other way around. The best organization on government spending had a rotten record on the deficit outlook.

The most comprehensive and authoritative study of forecast accuracy confirms this erratic performance. The study, done by Victor Zarnowitz of Columbia University for the National Bureau of Economic Research and published in December 1982, was based on quarterly surveys conducted since 1968 by NBER and the American Statistical Association. These surveys cover more than 70 forecasting organizations and analyze the results for inflation, real growth, unemployment, nominal GNP, consumer expenditures on durable goods, and changes in business inventories.

Zarnowitz concluded, "It is difficult for most individuals to predict *consistently* better than the group.... For most people most of the time, the predictive record is spotty, with but transitory spells of relatively high accuracy."[2]

It is hard to find much encouragement there!

Exhibit   **Predictive accuracy of 44 leading economists
and forecasting organizations,** 1977-1983

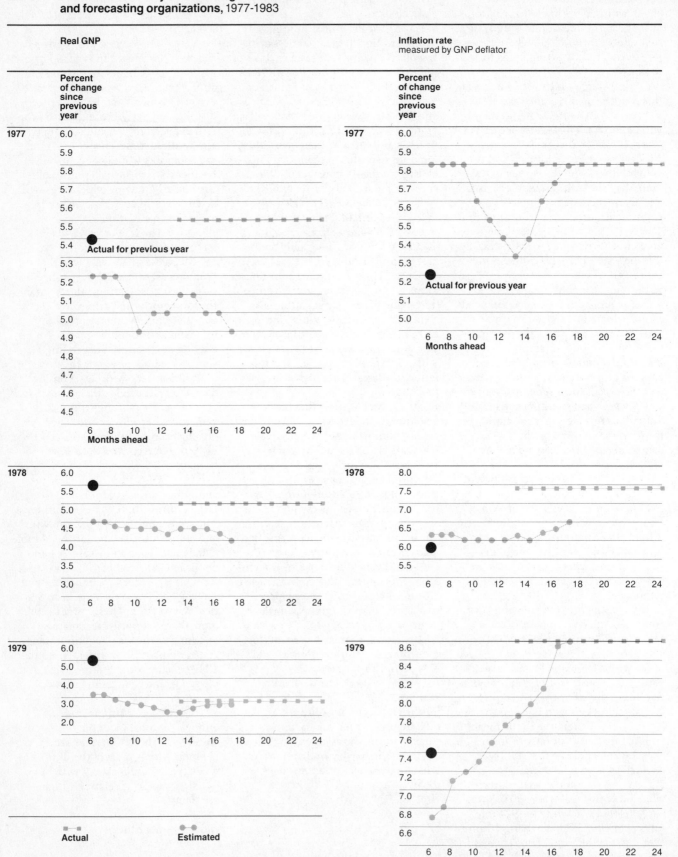

Real GNP

Percent
of change
since
previous
year

Inflation rate
measured by GNP deflator

Percent
of change
since
previous
year

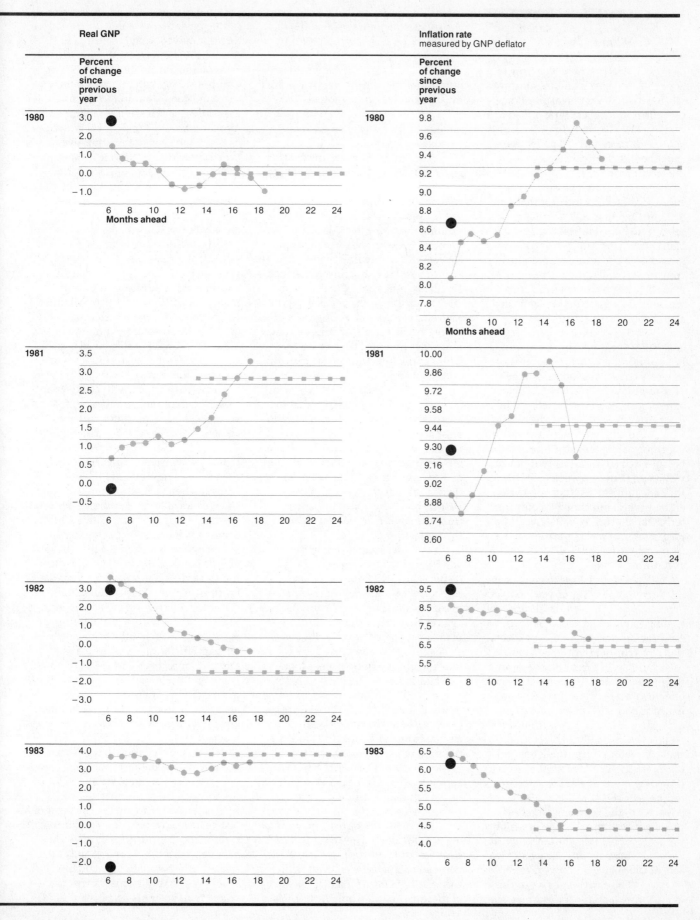

What to do?

There is, however, a ray of hope in Zarnowitz's finding: the probabilities are high that on average the consensus will be less wrong than one person's forecast, and almost certainly less wrong than ARIMA projections and other mechanical extrapolations of the recent past.

But is that prospect good enough? We want a forecast that will be right. One that is less wrong than another is no help if it bears little resemblance to what actually occurs. In answer to this objection, we present some convincing evidence that the errors made by consensus economic forecasts are small enough to make them valuable for business decisions.

This evidence comes from analysis of the Blue Chip Economic Indicators surveys, which show the monthly consensus forecast of the year-to-year percentage rate of change of principal economic variables. Unlike most surveys of this kind, the Blue Chip is broadly based with an unchanging group of respondents. Moreover, because it appears monthly, it reflects views less than two weeks old when they are published. Other surveys are either irregular in timing or only quarterly. Our analysis covered the group's predictions for real GNP and inflation (as measured by the GNP deflator) for 1977 through 1983.

Robert J. Eggert, chief economist of the Blue Chip survey (now 48 organizations), interviews his panel of leading economists and organizations early each month to get their expectations for year-over-year changes in each variable. For example, beginning in June 1980, each panel member goes on line for the 1981 outlook; the published survey shows the predictions of each participating organization and the group consensus. The panelists continue to predict the outlook for 1981 until June 1981 rolls around, at which time they jump forward to an estimate for the year ahead, or 1982. And so on. (We refer to the year being forecast as the target year and the year in which the process begins as the current year.)

In analyzing the results we sought the answers to two questions:

Did early forecasts, or those made before January of the target year, at least indicate whether production and inflation would show greater or smaller rates of change than the current year?

Did successive monthly projections move deliberately toward the ultimately correct figure or did they wander away from it or move in random fashion as the target year approached its midpoint?

The accompanying charts give the answers. Each diagram in the *Exhibit* shows the year-over-year percentage change from the current year to the target year as a horizontal line running from Month 13 through Month 24. The monthly prediction appears as a wiggly line beginning with Month 6 and running through Month 17 (that is, June through May). The large black dot on the vertical axis of each chart shows the average rate of change of the variable during the current year – included to indicate whether the forecasters were expecting a stronger or a weaker year to come.

Each year has its own peculiarities, but the overall record is impressive. The group shows an average error of only 1.1 percentage points between the October forecast of real GNP for the target year and the actual figure. By and large the early forecasts capture the directional change from the current year. By and large, with the passage of time, the consensus does move toward the actual figure.

The second year in the survey, 1978, turned out to have the worst record. The GNP forecast looks outrageously low, but extensive revisions in the National Income Accounts after 1978 changed the original official estimate for 1978 GNP from 4.4% above 1977's to 5.0%. This alteration explains why the Blue Chip consensus looks so stubbornly low.

The inflation forecast, however, has no such excuse. Here the group persisted in predicting little change from 1977 when in fact the inflation rate moved from less than 6% to 7.4%. Only late in the game, in the spring of 1978, did the panel reluctantly – and much too timidly – raise its sights toward reality.

The economists' predictions for 1979 look better, even though the early inflation forecast was far off the mark and actually set a lower figure than the 1978 rate. A regular follower of these estimates would nevertheless have noted the steep and persistent rise in the projection for inflation, as the forecast moved from 6.7% in June 1978 to about 7.7% in December and then right on the button by May 1979. Furthermore, as we can see, the group was early and consistent in recognizing that the intensification of inflationary pressures would dampen real growth.

In each of the other five years, the early forecast either spotted the right direction or quickly corrected itself when it was wrong. Thus, by the end of the current year a good sense of the character of the target year had already been established.

Note the phrase "a good sense of the character of the target year." In view of all the uncertainties surrounding any business decision, managers will care very little whether the outlook for real growth is 4.5% or 5.5% or the outlook for inflation is 6.2% or 6.9%. What they need is a sense of whether the overall level of business activity will be rising or falling, whether the pace will be faster or slower than in the current year, and whether the environment will encourage aggressive or cautious pricing.

In this context, we suggest that these consensus forecasts satisfy executives' requirements. That is so even when economic conditions change radically, as they did in 1982.

In mid-1981 the Blue Chip consensus failed to recognize that a recession lay just ahead or that the rate of inflation was on the verge of collapsing. Give the economists black marks for those errors. On the other hand, the group did start off by forecasting a lower rate of inflation in 1982 – though it did underestimate the degree of change. Furthermore, although the forecast for real GNP in 1982 remained positive until January of that year, it moved downward persistently and at an accelerated rate during November and December, by which time both the real GNP forecast and the inflation forecast were signaling that 1982 would be radically different from 1981.

The predictions for 1983 also deserve comment. Admittedly, most forecasters failed to foresee the vigor of last year's recovery. Can you fault that error when, in mid-1982, close to the very depths of the recession and some five months before the trough, this group was unambiguously expecting a recovery in business activity in 1983?

The economists were less aggressive early on in projecting the rapid decline in inflation, which actually fell to 4.2% from 6.0% in 1982 and 9.4% in 1981; but their estimate declined steadily and with growing momentum during the second half of 1982.

Is it all too easy?

Some people have argued—Milton Friedman has argued vociferously—that there is nothing impressive about this record. They maintain that forecasting rates of change from this year's level to next year's should be a cinch and that the increasing accuracy of estimates as we move into the target year should be no surprise.

After all, we begin the game with the information on this year's conditions. As time passes, what is known increases and the projection element diminishes. As Friedman put it in recent correspondence, "It would be absolutely astounding if the error did not tend to decrease as the period of time went on....[The forecaster] needs to know less and less because more and more is already known."

Friedman's point is indisputable. Its significance for the usefulness of systematic and regular consensus forecast surveys, however, is something else again.

It would of course be preferable if the Blue Chip economists were willing to put their names to forecasts running from the current quarter to, say, four quarters ahead, in which case little known information would be used. While the Blue Chip indicators do show forecasts of that type, Eggert attaches no names of organizations to the quarterly forecasts on the basis that they are indeed likely to have larger margins of error. It is a fair guess that these forecasters would take more care in arriving at the numbers attached to their names than in furnishing numbers published anonymously.

The evidence we have given is impressive nonetheless because even the early forecasts—those made during the latter half of the current year—were largely accurate in direction. As most corporate managers make their plans for the coming year during the autumn of the current year, those early indica-

tions can make an important contribution to the planning process.

Does anyone care?

Is all this an intellectual exercise, or does it matter? To put the question differently, can you run a business successfully without making judgments about what the future will look like?

The answer to the second question is obvious. On the other hand, the quality of those judgments is dubious. Many business executives nurse painful memories of inventories urgently accumulated just before all the orders vanished, of irreplaceable employees laid off just before the customers started flocking back, of plants built in expectation of ever-rising sales that failed to materialize, and of prices raised so high that the company lost business to competitors.

The factor that makes these errors common is the human tendency to expect tomorrow to look like today or, worse, to extend today's trends out to tomorrow. Change is not only unwelcome; it is also difficult to visualize. The unfortunate consequence is that surprise continually overtakes us.

Indeed, the business cycle itself, despite its varied roots, is in many ways a process in which corporations join one another in overdoing their optimism and pessimism and then having to correct their errors. Inventory ordering, borrowing, pricing, employment, and capital spending run to unsustainable heights and then fall to unsustainable lows.

The attempts of each business to correct its excesses in one direction or the other only make matters worse for the other businesses that are trying to do the same thing at the same time. Obviously, corporate executives are not paying attention to the economic consensus.

But we all do listen to forecasts in one form or another. Some of us listen to customers or competitors. Some heed our friendly bankers. Many sit up and take notice when a Wall Street guru predicts Armageddon or nirvana. One or another of these forecasts will often be correct, but none of them has enough consistency to meet

even the crudest tests of statistical significance. Which means that most of the time they supply noise, not information.

Nevertheless, early warning of change is essential to avoid being caught in the gales that blow through the economy. Reliable forecasts that tell us we are approaching the late stages of an expansion or the early stages of a recession can lead us to act in anticipation of those developments and, in the process, to avoid the excesses that cause them. If such is the case, we should listen to sources that are sensitive to the development of unsustainable rates of growth or shrinkage in the economy—sources that understand the cyclical process and can recognize how it has been evolving.

This is what economists are trained to do. While the record suggests that they have less consistency as forecasters than each of them (or we!) would like to have, the law of large numbers works in their favor. We should bet with the consensus. ▽

Reprint 84503